PENGUIN BOOKS

MRS FUNNYBONES

Twinkle Khanna, aka Mrs Funnybones, crafts satirical stories and funny fables when she is not running a design business, selling candles or running in circles around her small but rather odd family. She narrowly escaped a gruesome tragedy when Bollywood tried to bludgeon her brain to the size of a pea, but she ducked at the right moment and escaped, miraculously unharmed. She is a popular columnist and a regular contributor to the *Times of India* and *DNA After Hrs*. Currently, she is in the process of creating lame jokes like, 'Why do all Hindu boys worship their mother? Because their religion tells them to worship the cow.' She firmly believes that nothing in life is sacred except laughter.

Mrs Funnybones

SHE'S JUST
LIKE YOU
AND A LOT
LIKE ME

Twinkle Khanna

PENGUIN BOOKS

An imprint of Penguin Random House

PENGUIN BOOKS

USA | Canada | UK | Ireland | Australia
New Zealand | India | South Africa | China

Penguin Books is part of the Penguin Random House group of companies
whose addresses can be found at global.penguinrandomhouse.com

Published by Penguin Random House India Pvt. Ltd
7th Floor, Infinity Tower C, DLF Cyber City,
Gurgaon 122 002, Haryana, India

First published by Penguin Books India 2015

Illustrations by Kruttika Susarla
Some of these pieces have appeared in a slightly different form in the *Times of
India, DNA After Hrs* and other publications.

37

The views and opinions expressed in this book are the author's own and the facts
are as reported by her which have been verified to the extent possible, and the
publishers are not in any way liable for the same.

ISBN 9780143424468

Text design by Vedanti Sikka
Typeset in Sabon by R. Ajith Kumar, New Delhi
Printed at Thomson Press India Ltd, New Delhi

www.penguin.co.in

For my Dad

CONTENTS

CONTENTS

FOREWORD

First things first, am I exactly like the woman in the book that you are about to read? Not entirely, she is slightly lazier, a bit more high-strung and her jokes are a lot funnier than mine.

In writing her and the characters around her, I have thrown in a few facts, a little fiction, a few decaying brain cells and a couple of old bones into my brewing cauldron of words.

It all started with Sarita Tanwar asking me if I would write a humorous weekly column for her newspaper. Her exact words were: 'You crack daft jokes all the time and you read incessantly, I am sure you can write.'

I tried telling her that millions of people watch cricket all the time but I doubt if they can play, but she interrupted me by saying that I should write a piece and then we shall see.

What did I really know about writing? Memories of a half-written book in my teens surfaced; this, along with a file of morbid poems, all focusing on death and maggots, constituted my entire writing experience.

But I have always had a peculiar way of looking at life, and my goal to amuse myself often ended up amusing others as well.

In my opinion, growing older is all about learning and passing it on, otherwise there is no reason for biological evolution to keep us alive after our reproductive years are over.

A clearer view of life is probably the only silver lining to having to hoist your boobs over your shoulder and getting to the point where not only do you have eye bags, but even your eye bags begin to sag.

So, having fulfilled my function of ensuring that the population of India continues to explode, and before dementia sets in, I decided to sit down, open my laptop and start my first column, which led to almost a hundred columns, and then it eventually brought me right here, to this very book.

Now, this is the time to turn the page and dive into Mrs Funnybones (the book, you twits, not me!).

Starring 'you know who' as the main lead, then of course, the man of the house, the eccentric mothers, two fairly strange children, and cameos by stubborn canines, weird neighbours, Parsi electricians and even a movie star or two. Welcome to my world . . .

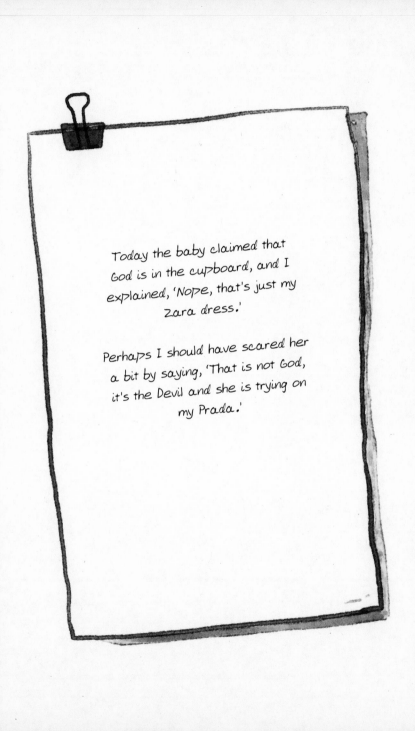

Today the baby claimed that God is in the cupboard, and I explained, 'Nope, that's just my Zara dress.'

Perhaps I should have scared her a bit by saying, 'That is not God, it's the Devil and she is trying on my Prada.'

A: AM I AN IDIOT?

8 a.m.: The prodigal son, the baby and I are wildly dancing to 'All about that bass', a song that primarily deals with the concept that a big backside is infinitely better, and since the baby can also just about warble through the chorus, this is immediately declared our favourite song of all time. The radio plays on and there is the notorious *Anaconda* song again about having a big booty, and when the baby starts trying to mouth, 'Oh my God, look at her butt', an observation that

may not go down so well with her playschool teachers, I hastily switch the music off.

9 a.m.: Trying to check my emails, I get hold of my iPad and boom there it is: #breaktheinternet and pictures of Kim Kardashian pouring champagne while balancing a glass on her bottom. Kimmy darling, why didn't you tell me you wanted a drink? You really didn't need to pose as a human bar counter; I would have just sent my Ramu and Pappu. One would hold the glass, the other would pour and you could sit, relax and use your posterior to break the sofa instead.

To digress a little, before the world even knew Kimmy existed, we had the famous choreographer Saroj Khan who could certainly balance a tray and a cup of tea on her bottom if she tried, not that she ever did. She used that bit to sway gloriously and teach others to do the same. Just like our politicians, I am bringing this up to prove that anything anyone

4

can do, we Indians could have or have done it earlier and better.

As I am formulating the rest of my patriotic speech, I hear the man of the house say, 'Can you be quiet for just five minutes?' And I realize that I have actually been speaking aloud while hunched over my iPad. Blimey . . .

11 a.m.: Sitting in front of my computer and drinking coffee, I spot an email from my accountant stating, 'Dear Madam, My sister very dangerous. I want to saw her. Please give leave three days! Good day, Srinivasan'

Hmm . . . Either his sister is a serial killer and he has decided to cut her in half or as I quickly figure (with the help of a strong swig of coffee), he is saying that his sister is sick and he wants to see her.

I send him an email back informing him that since this is his nineteenth relative in grave danger, he needs to either consult a tantric to remove a curse on his family or to simply stop lying to take extra days off. I shut my computer and hurriedly get ready to reach the office.

4 p.m.: I am at the store and we are launching our new collection when I notice that instead of dealing with a customer who will hopefully spend all her husband's hard-earned money on my beautiful, gold-embossed candles, my salesgirl is fast asleep at her desk. I tentatively wipe drool from the cash register and give her a sharp nudge. She yelps awake and then gives me her sorry tale of being sleep deprived due to her husband's daily sonorous and torturous snoring. Blimey . . .

7.45 p.m.: Mother has come over for a cup of tea, and as we are chatting, the prodigal son runs into the room and yells that he needs to buy a book urgently for his English assignment. Crossword is the nearest bookstore, so we quickly decide to go there. I grab my bag with one hand, lug the baby with the other and hurriedly ask mom to drop us off at the store while leaving instructions with the watchman to inform our driver to reach Crossword in twenty minutes.

8.10 p.m.: We are at the bookstore and I tell the prodigal son, 'Hey, let's go to that aisle, I need some pens and I can see some marker pens there.' And the baby immediately chirps, 'Where pens? Show me!' She is at such a precious age; curious about everything. We buy two books on poetry for the prodigal son and a Dora sticker book for the baby and head out.

Standing on the dark pavement, I am scanning the street for my car to no avail. I try calling the driver but the number is unreachable, and after fifteen minutes of being stared at by passers-by with the baby squirming in my arms, the prodigal son says that he sees a rickshaw. The baby squeaks, 'Where rickshaw? Show me!'

8.30 p.m.: The prodigal son hails the rickshaw and we all clamber in. This is the baby's first ride in a rickshaw and she is rather thrilled. We then turn into the long private road that leads to our building when the rickshaw driver suddenly says, 'Madam, that hero Akshay Kumar used to live here but now he lives in Bandra.'

As my mouth falls open and before I can protest, he continues, 'Arrey, he's married to Rajesh Khanna's daughter, na, and Dimple

Kapadia is there but the daughter doesn't have anything to do with the mother; especially now that she is the only heir. So this Akshay and his family have all moved to that big house in Bandra.'

Bemused with the nonsense this moronic man is spouting, I say, 'Really? And how would you know that?' Pat comes the answer, *'Madam, rickshaw chalata hun, sab pata hain.'* (We rickshaw drivers know everything.)

The prodigal son starts laughing hysterically as I struggle to pull out my fare of seventeen rupees, and we run up the stairs to our house.

The man of the house is sprawled on the couch and I breathlessly start narrating the whole sequence. 'So funny! Listen, na, apparently Akshay Kumar used to live here but now he lives in Bandra and his wife hates her mother and . . .'

The man of the house narrows his eyes and exclaims, 'You were heading towards it but now you have gone certifiably insane. What are you babbling about Akshay and his wife and her mother? That's us, our family! Who refers to their entire family in the third person? You are really an idiot.'

I immediately correct him. 'The word is not idiot but illeist. Illeist is a person who talks in the third person, whereas an idiot just talks; though they sound similar, they cannot be used in place of each other.'

Shrugging his shoulders and giving me a goofy grin, he retorts, 'I don't know what an illeist is but I know an idiot when I see one.'

The baby immediately stops playing with her tea set, looks up and says, 'Where idiot? Show me!'

Blimey . . .

Nothing is free in life except
bad advice.

B: BEWARE OF MOMMY DEAREST

My mother has never been the Band-Aid dispensing, cupcake-baking, checking-on-homework sort of mother that one sees in commercials. She is funny, sometimes wacky, a little eccentric and fallibly human, and has consistently over the years found new and unique ways to embarrass me, starting at birth when she decided that naming me Twinkle was a foolproof way of making sure that I would get teased throughout my life, have immigration officers at various airports stare at my passport and shake with hysterical laughter and strangers stalk me with WhatsApp messages like, 'Twinkle, Twinkle, little star, I hope you get hit by a car!'

Here is a short list of the things that she has done to traumatize me at various stages.

I AM THIRTEEN: I am studying at Panchgani and have been selected to play in the inter-school basketball match. Mother has come to see the match, as it is a big moment in my life. In the middle of the match, she starts yelling from the stands, 'Tina! Tina! You are the best!' and when I turn to hear where all this ruckus is coming from, the ball is thrown my way, smacks me on the head and I fall down flat on the court.

I AM EIGHTEEN: Mother has read a book on some colour therapy diet by Linda Clark, and decided that I must follow this innovative weight-loss programme which consists of eating only red- and orange-coloured fruits, drinking solarized water in red bottles and sitting in front of an infrared light for fifteen minutes every day. End result after two weeks: I have gained 3 pounds and have a burn mark on my stomach from the infrared light toppling and falling on me.

I AM TWENTY-NINE: Mom and I are going to London for a shoot and Mom is then going on to New York while I am heading home. Every day mother goes shopping and as I see our tiny room filling up with shopping bags, I start getting a feeling that this will not end well. It is the last day, my flight is at 8 p.m. and mom's flight is four hours before mine. I start fretting as to how she will fit all her stuff in her suitcase and she reassures me that I have nothing to worry about—to go to work and she will pack everything for me as well before she leaves.

That evening I rush to my room to pick up my bags, only to find no suitcases, just two trunks. Description of the above-mentioned trunks: Dented, battered aluminium boxes with my name plastered across in massive letters and misspelt 'Twinkal Khana' with a bright red marker pen.

Mommy dearest has taken the two suitcases I had come with, to accommodate all the shopping and has packed all my things in the film unit's costume department trunks.

I AM THIRTY-SEVEN: My mother decides to call my entire family over for dinner—husband, in-laws, cousins and all—and then proceeds to talk about how fat I was as a child, how I got stuck in a bucket while trying to have a bath, how I used to eat mangoes sitting on the potty and how she had to buy clothes for a fourteen-year-old when I was just seven.

And then last week . . .

8 a.m.: My phone rings, it is mother, and she says, 'I saw your console table in the foyer yesterday, it's the first thing guests will see when they enter your house and it is looking very empty. You need to buy an antique statue and place it there immediately.'

I need to nip this potentially long conversation in the bud quickly, so I reply, 'Granny is antique too, let's make her sit on the console whenever guests come by.'

Mommy dearest hangs up without a word.

1.30 p.m.: Mother has forgotten all about our morning spat, and calls me in high spirits. She informs me that an old acquaintance from Delhi is coming over this evening. The lady in question has been trying to persuade mommy dearest to partake in a great money-making scheme, and mom has already decided that it is a fabulous opportunity and is now persuading me to take advantage of her friend's generous offer.

6 p.m.: Our much-awaited visitor arrives. She is articulate, intelligent and extremely charming. I am almost convinced that I must part with most of my money, when I start mentally doing some calculations and an alarm bell starts ringing. I protest that nothing in the world can help you earn 125 per cent per annum, especially when the bank is just about giving 9 per cent. Every question I ask is met with vague answers

like angel investors, trading in yen, etc. till the meeting comes to an abrupt end.

8.30 p.m.: My mother receives an SMS from her friend, which states, 'I am very disappointed with your daughter's attitude. What does she keep mumbling percentages for? Does she even know what she is saying? Under these conditions I take back my kind offer of granting you a place in my scheme. It's your loss.'

Mother starts berating me for having spoilt this great prospect and when I try explaining to her that this is just a money-making racket as the numbers don't add up, she again yells at me for behaving like I am 'some kind of maths teacher'. Hurt about the maths dig, I remind her that I had scored 97 out of 100 in my board exams on the same subject. She must remember that at least, since she and my aunt had made fun of me saying, 'The Human Calculator not only gets 97 marks but also weighs 97 kilos.'

She gets even more irked, so I sneakily grab her phone and send her friend a message back: 'CBI has just arrested MP Ramchandra and two ex-MLAs in a Ponzi scheme, would you like to join them?'

A month later, mom calls me and says, 'I have been trying our Delhi friend's number but she hasn't returned my calls. Really, you should have been nicer to her. Didn't even serve her biscuits properly with tea that day. But I agree with you, it's better to be safe than sorry. What is too good to be true usually is . . . Anyway, listen, I got a letter from a nice Nigerian man who wants to give us some money . . .'

Before she can continue, I yell, 'Oh my God!' She starts giggling and says, 'I am just joking.' I tell her, 'It's not funny, Mom, and sometimes you really do make stupid mistakes.'

She snorts, 'That's true, I made you.'

THE PARSI CONNECTION

This year I ordered my son's birthday cake from Mrs Byramjee and when I told her that I'd be sending my driver to pick it up, she informed me, 'Send a young driver only.' My mind was filled with risqué thoughts of what this eighty-year-old wanted to do with my driver, and when I asked her, she snapped at me, so I sent my twenty-two-year-old cousin (since he is the youngest man I know with a driving licence). When he got back, he said that she pinched his cheek, gave him a toothless grin and simply handed the cake over. I am still trying to figure that one out.

GETTING READY FOR AN EVENT

Me: My leg is hurting, should I skip wearing heels today?

My Parsi assistant: It's fine, ma'am, even the men are wearing flats.

C: CAN INDIAN MEN CONTROL ANYTHING BESIDES THEIR WIVES?

7 a.m.: I feel a sharp tug on my nose and suddenly something damp and smelly falls on my face. As I struggle to open my eyes, I realize that it is in fact my daughter who is struggling to put her finger up my nose in anticipation of perhaps finding a brain wedged in there somewhere, and to free herself from all encumbrances in this fruitful task, she has removed her overnight diaper and thrown it on my forehead.

8.45 a.m.: I grab some coffee and decide to get a head start on my day by jotting down my to-do list.

TO-DO TODAY

1. Remove brownie stains from the sofa.

2. Remove stains from my new pants when I sat on the brownie on the sofa.

3. Box son on the head for saying he stored the brownie behind the cushion on the sofa for safekeeping.

4. Delete twenty-six pictures of cousin Kamalnath (Sweetie) Khanna and his family that have very sweetly been emailed to me.

5. Delete seventy-three early morning 'inspirational' SMS forwards that only deranged people have the inclination to send.

6. Call the lawyer to check on my court case regarding my (tied-to-a-tree) dog managing to bite our nasty neighbour—double check if I can file a counter case against our nasty neighbour for violating the dog's personal

nasal space by regularly stinking of methi *theplas*, thereby provoking the dog into a biting frenzy due to temporary insanity.

11 a.m.: I am sitting at my desk trying to figure out if I can miraculously convert a 2000-square-foot space in Khar into some version of a Venetian villa that my client insists is the only thing that can satisfy his vision of a perfect home. These are the moments when I wish my name was Twinkbaba and I could hypnotize my annoying client into letting me simply do my job.

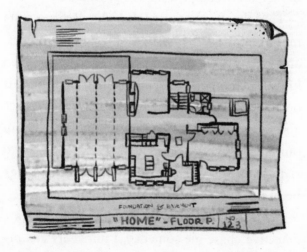

1 p.m.: Mrs Irani, my electrical contractor, comes into my cabin. She is a sweet Parsi lady and one of the few women contractors in her field.

I had spoken to her a few weeks ago when she called to complain that one of our clients had not paid her for her work. I told her that I was unable to help her as he had gypped me of my fees as well.

Today she is grinning and holding her cheque. She tells me that she got our client followed by a private detective and when she threatened to reveal all his slightly illegal activities, he immediately coughed up our payment.

I am shocked because I thought all this private investigator stuff happens only in the movies, and as I am wondering how she would even know such a person, she tells me, 'Bhabhi, this detective was involved in my friend's divorce and I kept good relations with him. After all, in our business you meet so many types—*sanghrelo saap bi koi divas kaam aave* (even a snake may be useful someday).

Wondering if she would make her private detective chase me someday, I hurriedly ask my accountant to clear an outstanding payment we owe her of Rs 250 for a single light bulb. One never knows what can make these people blow their fuse.

3 p.m.: I ask the site supervisor for the weekly report of completed tasks and this is what I get instead:

1. The painter was supposed to produce an ash-grey paint sample today but can't because his bua's uncle has to move from some Campa Cola building, and of course, the whole clan has to pitch in.

2. Our wood carver's mother's sister's daughter's cousin is getting married, so work on my Gothic chairs will not start for another three weeks.

3. The head plumber is missing two days this week because of Bakri Eid.

4. The entire carpentry team is absconding for Lakshmi puja because they are all brothers as they live in neighbouring villages (which

is apparently as close a mental–physical bond as being conjoined twins).

4 p.m.: I throw yet another cup of coffee down my throat and get into my Sherlock Holmes mode to discover why we are paying Rs 43 more per kg of wax than required and is it a genuine oversight or does my purchase manager need a few whacks from our good old Mumbai policemen.

6.30 p.m.: I have come to meet my new clients at their home which even at first glance needs severe redecoration. I am sitting on a rather uncomfortable chair at their hideous dining table and facing the middle-aged couple who are explaining their requirements for the project.

The husband fetches the architectural plans of the house and comes next to my chair. He bends over trying to unroll the plans on the table, and the motion dislodges the intestinal gas which till this moment has been probably lying dormant inside his posterior (which by the way, is four inches away from my face) and lets out a noisy, flatulent missile. I almost choke on the noxious odour but the couple just continue the conversation as if nothing out of the ordinary has just transpired. It takes all my years of yoga training to maintain a straight face and I hurriedly finish the meeting. Their secretary ushers me to the main door and just as I am leaving, I overhear the mistress of the house screech at her husband, 'Pintu, not fair, bad manners to behave like this, little control, please!'

He yells back, 'Yaar, you say the same line in the bedroom also. Sex and gas even God can't control.'

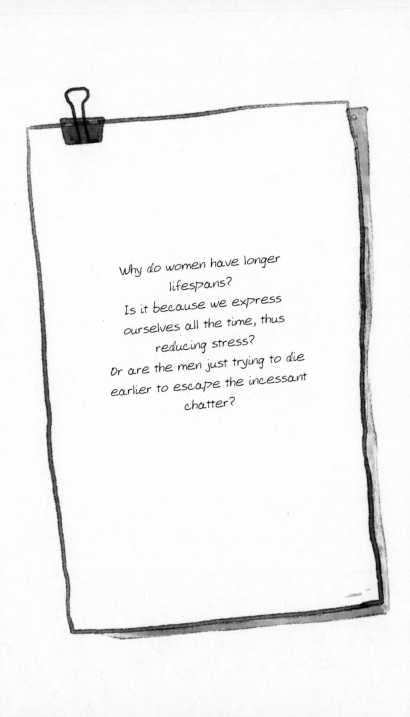

Why do women have longer
lifespans?
Is it because we express
ourselves all the time, thus
reducing stress?
Or are the men just trying to die
earlier to escape the incessant
chatter?

D: DOING THE
DAUGHTER-IN-LAW THING

Mummyji is what everyone calls my mother-in-law. She is fierce, formidable and fiery, hence a bit like me in some ways and radically different in others.

When I was a newly-wed, she sat me down and explained, 'Two tigers cannot live in the same field.' I was a bit puzzled as I had no idea that she was an animal conservationist. When I kept asking the man of the house about her work with wildlife welfare groups, he gave me a withering look and said, 'She means you and she can't live in the same field.' I just shrugged my shoulders and said, 'No sweat off my back, darling, as I live on the first floor, she can have the field all to herself.'

But gradually, I realized that mummyji was right; we would be sharing the same field, though not as tigers but as the main cheerleaders for the one man out there who technically belongs to both of us; so we might as well shake our pom-poms together. Which is precisely what a good mother-in-law–daughter-in-law relationship truly is.

All you mummyjis beware! If your daughter-in-law claims that she loves you like her own mother, then *daal mein kuch kaala hai* and that little black spot could very well be rat poison.

One day over lunch with a few girlfriends, we started talking about mothers-in-law and I jotted down a few of their stories.

Friend No. 1 said that when she was pregnant, her mother-in-law gave her a picture of Lord Krishna to gaze at since this would help produce a bonny boy. When she produced a beautiful, dusky baby girl, mother-in-law was aghast. Friend no. 1 said, 'Mummy, looking at the picture every day didn't help in making the baby a boy, but it sure gave her Krishna's colour.' Mother-in-law at that point promptly collapsed.

Friend No. 2 recalled that when she was newly married, she went to have tea with her mother-in-law, who remarked that her beloved son was looking a bit grubby and to send him to mommy so that she can scrub him with her own hands till he shines. (A fine idea when he was six but at thirty-six this was way beyond creepy.)

Friend No. 3 had a mother-in-law (past tense doesn't mean she is dead, just that my friend had the sense to divorce both her and her son) who decided that her nine-month pregnant bahu breaking her water bag was not a sign to rush to the hospital. Maji proceeded to have dinner and after leisurely having dessert, announced that it was perhaps now time to leave for the hospital.

Friend No. 4 is always complaining that her mother-in-law criticizes her, nudges her out of family pictures, grabs the front seat next to her beloved son in the car and keeps repeating how Shonu (some kind of gross childhood nickname, I assume) loves mommy more than anyone else.

Friend No. 5 is convinced that her mother-in-law has bribed her staff. The moment she locks the bedroom door with her husband, ready for some action, mummyji promptly calls on the intercom asking for her darling son to come visit.

We spent the afternoon amidst uproarious laughter and I probably would have continued making digs at all the mummyjis for the next decade, but last week I woke up to this:

8 a.m.: In the midst of stifling a yawn and pulling my dog out from his favourite hiding place, my

phone rings. It's my mother-in-law and she has a complaint, 'Beta, he came up to the house yesterday, he has become so thin, why are you not feeding him properly?' I am a bit confused because I have been feeding the dog the same thing for years and he seems to look pretty much the same to me. As I start protesting, she adds, 'His favourite dish as a child was *makki di roti* and *sarson da saag*, I will make it for him today. He is looking very *kamzor*.' Ahhh . . . I get it. She is talking about the man of the house.

A Punjabi mother, her son and food form a triad as sacred as Brahma, Mahesh and Vishnu, and cannot be interfered with as I learnt in the early years of my marriage.

I want to tell her that the man of the house has deliberately lost eight kilos for his next role as a wiry boxer but it's just nicer to let her send the makki di roti and the saag, especially since it's my all-time favourite dish as well.

3 p.m.: An old friend from my boarding school days is in town and she drops by for coffee. I don't see her very often, though we catch each other

on Facebook occasionally, but that comfort of having known each other our entire lives never seems to go away.

I giggle and tell her about my morning makki di roti story, and she just starts ranting, 'Last week on Zee TV, I saw Modi asking everyone to sweep places, all these movie stars and all . . . so exciting, na? I went to Star Bazaar to get the monthly ration and I also bought two new brooms, but mummyji snapped at me, saying that I don't understand anything—it is only a symbol to clean India. I told her, "Then why are we not using symbol to clean the house? Tell me, Mummyji, why are we using big vacuum cleaner to clean our house if symbol can clean the whole of India?"

'Mummyji always wants to show everyone how we are so modern with all these different machines and all—if we are modern people, we would use only iPhone 6, not all these other cheapo phones. She thinks from my room I can't see her on the balcony, but I can! Always sitting, drinking coffee and reading *Economic Times*. At this age, she should be reading Bhagavad Gita or newspaper, you tell me?'

I am staring at her in shock and horror because . . .

I have this vision where our son will finally get his wife home. She will place hideous red cushions on my sofas, never polish my silver tea set, will feed my son his favourite fried chicken by actually deep-frying it and not in the Philips (oil-free airfryer) machine like I do, and she will stare at me when I am sitting in the balcony, drinking copious amounts of coffee and reading my Asimovs . . . because one day soon enough I will be a mummyji too.

One always looks at this age-old mother-in-law–daughter-in-law battle from the daughter-in-law's point of view, but I realize it must not be easy to be mummyji as well.

I hastily whip out my phone and delete the mother-in-law joke that I had made up and posted on Facebook: 'God could not be everywhere, so He created mothers, and the Devil could not be everywhere, so He created mothers-in-law.' And I upload my new motto, 'Do unto another as you would want the (future) other to do unto you.'

Son: Can I pack my Nerf Gun?
Me: Sure! And when they arrest you at the airport, you can shoot them and run away.
Son: Your jokes suck, Mom.

Son: Why is the Wi-Fi not working?
Me: Mansukh bhai, the Internet guy, has been assassinated by school moms.
Son: Daad! Can't take this any more!

E: EUREKA! MOM, I CAN MAKE ANYONE PREGNANT NOW!

8.15 a.m.: The man of the house is leaving for a shoot to Pune and he appoints the prodigal son as 'safety officer' in charge of looking after the baby and me.

1.30 p.m.: We are all watching the news together when we see our wonderful Parliament erupt in chaos and violence, with our beloved MPs taking out pen knives and pepper sprays.

1.45 p.m.: The prodigal son has been watching this very keenly and has now decided to take his position as 'safety officer' very seriously, and inspired by what we have just seen on screen, goes off looking for an old Swiss knife which was tucked away in the cupboard.

2 p.m.: The benefits of the Swiss knife have been discussed in depth and he has shown me detailed demonstrations of how it has scissors, a nail file, a saw, a knife and a bottle opener.

2.30 p.m.: The much-abused daybed in our house has suffered a minor mishap when the scissors from the Swiss knife got stuck in it, thereby not just tearing the fabric but also ripping the stuffing.

4 p.m.: The staff have come to complain that the great Swiss knife experiment is leading to mounting deaths and injuries among household items:

1. Mosquito net ripped.

2. Daybed damaged as mentioned above.

3. Olive oil bottle broken.

4. Dog's hair trimmed only near the right ear.

5. Our son's hair trimmed only near his left ear.

6. The baby's favourite doll fatally stabbed.

Not to forget our watchman who has been threatened with the 'saw' component of the magnificent Swiss implement to ensure that he does not let unknown visitors into our house.

I am dismayed and give him a piece of my mind by yelling, 'There is no difference between you and the members of the Indian Parliament, all that's left for you to do is to take a can of pepper spray and violently spray it on our neighbour's face!' Oops . . .

4.15 p.m.: Our son has now googled the above-mentioned incident on YouTube and after again seeing how effective the pepper spray is when used by a particular MP, has decided to make his own version:

INGREDIENTS

1 empty spray bottle
500 ml of water
4 tablespoons of lemon juice
14 spoons of red chilli powder
8 spoons of salt

4.50 p.m.: I have now confiscated all potential weapons from his arsenal.

5 p.m.: I am frantically begging the man of the house to talk to his son and put some sense in his head, but the man of the house firmly denies any responsibility in this particular fiasco and instead points out that if the highest citizens in our country can contribute to violence in the Parliament, then how can our son be blamed for the violence in our house.

After seeing the validity of his point and realizing that in order to join the Parliament, you don't need to be a graduate or have any particular qualifications barring eligible age, I have decided that in exactly fourteen years our son can become an MP but perhaps he has to practise a few more parliamentary actions like yelling incoherently, breaking tables, snatching papers and smashing mikes, to really fit in.

Meanwhile, I need to practise removing stains from furniture, as that seems to be my primary occupation at home. I scrub away, thinking of ways to remove the prodigal son from his position as baby Ganpati standing outside his mom's house, because if something happens to him, I don't think I can find an elephant head in time to make him my little Ganesha. Parvati had divine powers to join the head with her son's body whereas I will have to plonk an orange pumpkin on top of his torso and try my luck with spit and good old Fevicol.

5.30 p.m.: I hit upon a solution to my Ganpati problem by dragging the prodigal son into the house and forcing him to do some more homework.

7 p.m.: I am working on a few yoga poses and have finally managed to hoist my body into some version of a headstand when the prodigal son returns and loftily announces, 'Mom, I can make anyone pregnant now!' I violently choke, lose my balance and tumble onto the carpet.

At a loss for words for the first time in fifteen years, I feebly mutter, 'Uh, I don't think, er . . . you should do such things; it's not the right uhm . . . time and uh . . . the girl and you uh . . .'

'Yuck, that's gross, Mom!' he shrieks. 'You always think of such dirty things! I don't even talk to girls though you keep insisting that soon I will be running after them. I didn't mean it like that! Eww! I was doing some research for a school project and the youngest boy who has made anyone pregnant is eleven! The Internet says it's a world record, that's all. Dad is right! You say gross things all the time!' And the prodigal son storms off. Yikes!

NEIGHBOURS

Taking rounds of the building garden in my perpetual 'lose the last 5 pounds' mission, I see my elderly neighbour sitting on the grass and looking up at our building. He is not blinking, and drool is running out of his mouth. Worried that he may have suffered an epileptic fit, I run towards him, only to discover that he is staring at the silhouette of an undressed neighbour who has forgotten to draw her curtains. I decide to immediately warn my neighbour. I whip out my phone and, to my horror, she starts coming even closer to the window and now can be seen clearly, stark naked, and when she picks up the phone, I discover that this is partly my fault as her phone was lying on the window ledge and she has been fully exposed as she was trying to get to her phone, which has been ringing incessantly, due to 'Good Samaritan' me. Yikes!

F: FITNESS MANIA SPREADS IN THE BUILDING

The man of the house, unlike me, can actually cook. You must always find a partner who can do a few mundane chores around the house so that you can relax in your favourite armchair and nourish your brain with books just like these. If you do know how to cook, it is rather useful to pretend otherwise, unless you want to be periodically nagged by snotty children to make their messy and time-consuming favourite dishes right up to the day you get Alzheimer's and luckily forget the recipe along with your name.

I would rather take a nap on the balcony in the time that it takes to make complicated things like spaghetti Bolognese but that could just be due to the fact that I am always chronically sleep deprived and my entire day whizzes by running in circles, occasionally running on the treadmill and invariably running into odd situations . . .

TODAY

6.30 a.m.: I am wide awake as the man of the house has switched on all the lights and decided that this is the precise moment that he needs to further perfect his body, by a series of complex exercises that involve carrying his body weight on his right elbow. He cheerfully asks me to join him.

As much as I admire his zeal for self-inflicted punishment, the debate on whether to partake in his innovative routine or jab my eye three times instead is very short. The latter less-painful option accomplished, I decide to get out of bed and get a head start to my day.

7 a.m.: My body needs caffeine to lubricate all my joints into some semblance of normal function, but as I walk to the kitchen, the two children that at some mistaken point I deemed necessary for my happiness dash into me while playing 'Catch the mosquito or catch dengue' (a game unique to Mumbai suburbs).

10 a.m.: Rushing to the office, I walk to the lift in my building, when I hear loud, crashing sounds come from the stairway. I poke my head forward, curious about the commotion. Lo and behold,

it is my neighbours Mrs C and Mrs M (wearing polyester-printed salwar kameez and gleaming white sneakers) rushing up the stairs to the third floor and then back down to the second, again and again.

Getting dizzy just looking at them, I call out, 'Mrs C, Mrs M, what are you guys doing?'

Mrs C ignores me (the same way she ignores my monthly messages asking her to make sure her dog doesn't defecate in the front yard. Last Diwali, I very kindly sent her a beautifully wrapped made-in-Japan poop-scooper but never even got a thank-you note).

Mrs M answers with a pant, 'We are doing exercises. You can see, no. Then why asking?'

Muttering under my breath that no amount of running up and down floors can dislodge the 100 theplas they eat at each meal, I roll my eyes and leave the building.

2 p.m.: Sitting at my store and going through accounts is a dreary task. Though I feel I may need some sort of injectable drug to get through the day, I settle for some coffee and continue

breaking my head with numbers that never seem to add up just right.

5 p.m.: Back home and with time to spare, I decide to take the baby (fondly referred to as the 'little beast') to my mother's house so that she can harass other members of the family besides me.

I get there and mother dearest is sitting with her close friend, Honey, and trying to call up their friend, Bubble. Honey! Bubble! Dimple!

Does anyone still wonder why I have been lumped with a name that rhymes with sprinkle and wrinkle?

I am then informed by my mother that her weekly task of torturing me by showing me strange sculptures that she excavates from unknown sources and then tries to place in precarious corners of my house, has unfortunately come to a halt because she has been very busy promoting her new movie. And as I am secretly praying that her promotional activities don't stop for a few more months, she informs me that I must not get very disheartened as she has spoken to an antique shop dealer who is sending a 7-foot statue of a one-armed woman to my house early next week.

6.30 p.m.: I am walking back into my building and am jostled by yet another elderly aunty walking up the stairs. Wondering about this fitness mania that has suddenly gripped my entire building, I spot the hunky movie star who has finally moved into his third-floor apartment in our building, and it all makes sense.

Holding the baby with one hand, I smile feebly and wave at him, when he walks up to me, punches me hard on the arm, and says, 'Do you know how many times you have beaten me up when we were kids?' I have absolutely no recollection of this as I had spent my entire childhood mercilessly beating up various pimpled boys, half of whom grew up to be very famous people.

Promising to send him my yummy dahi *tikki*s, I enter my foyer and meet the man of the house. When I tell him about bumping into our new neighbour and finding out that apparently I have beaten him up as well, the man of the house just sighs and says, 'What is new? You beat me up every day too, maybe you should open a new kind of acting school.'

I protest that I really can't act.

He adds, 'I know that, but you can claim to be a lucky mascot: A punch from Twinkle will make your stars sparkle!'

I feebly protest that this slogan doesn't really rhyme.

He shushes me and continues, 'There will be testimonials from all your former students.

'Like Farhan Akhtar: "Every time Ms Khanna beat me, I thought *Bhaag Farhan Bhaag*. That is why I was so good in *Bhaag Milkha Bhaag*. It was sheer practice."

'Karan Johar: "I am successful only because of Ms Khanna's regular thrashings. Every wallop I received, I said *Kuch Kuch Hota Hai* and that's how the idea of my first film was born."

'Hrithik Roshan: "I became the superhero of *Krrish* only because of Ms Khanna's punches. It left a deep scar on my mind and I decided to grow up and fight evil." And of course me,

Akshay Kumar: "I would be nothing without Ms Khanna. I learnt karate, taekwondo and parkour only because of her blessings in the form of slaps and boxes."'

When I object that everyone knows he was a martial arts expert even before he met me, he snorts, 'So what? You, anyway, want to take credit for everything, so take credit for this as well.'

I hit him on the head and pull him out to our porch. Feeling calmer after looking at the beautiful sea, I tell him, 'The sea looks so gorgeous, and say thank you to me—if I had not fought with the builder to lower the boundary wall, we would be looking at only concrete.'

The man of the house shakes his head and just walks off. So weird. Behaving like he has his periods or something; men are so strange sometimes, who can understand them!

THREE THINGS WOMEN
TALK ABOUT CONSTANTLY

1. Diet: Women talk about their diet incessantly because they are constantly trying to reach their ideal weight. Unfortunately, this is a number that most of us last saw on the scale when we were fourteen and are unlikely to see again unless we chop one leg off.

2. Other women: Every woman's favourite topic. It's very rare that a bunch of girls sitting together will not discuss another bunch of girls. These women are dissected thoroughly; after critiquing their morals, their lack of style, etc., the conversation will invariably end with 'But you know she's quite sweet.'

3. Men: The various significant others are discussed in depth. What he said, why he said it and five versions of what he actually meant. The ex-boyfriends are discussed every so often—they're of course, total losers leading a miserable existence without our amazing presence in their lives.

G: GOOD GRIEF! THIS WEIGHING SCALE MUST BE DEFECTIVE

8 a.m.: The holidays have ended, and after a month of indulging in endless desserts, I dust off my weighing scale and gingerly balance myself on it. The number flashes very dramatically in red. I stagger back almost as if I'd been shot by a sniper's bullet. I pick up the pieces of my shattered vanity and resolve to start yet another diet.

Weight is a tricky thing for me. In primary school I was the fattest girl in my class, and though decades have passed and I may no longer look like the fattest girl in the class, I haven't forgotten her. Just like a house is sometimes haunted by its previous occupants, I am also occasionally haunted by that little fat girl.

1.30 p.m.: I am meeting some of my close girlfriends for lunch, and invariably before we have even put our handbags down, the topic goes to our weight. One friend is congratulated for losing what seems like 350 grams since we last saw her; I moan about my dreadful extra 5 pounds, another says that she is also again on a diet, while yet another friend chirps in with an entire thirty-minute story about how she lost (wait for this) 1 kilo, and then her aunty died and she was so upset that she ate some ice cream and gained the momentous 1 kilo back (the aunty dying is just mentioned in passing. I still don't know the aunt's name or what she died of, but I do know that my friend ate a family pack of chikoo ice cream).

We quickly scan the menu and order dainty salads, and as we are about to finish, we undo all our good work by ordering cream cookies and cupcakes, and after oohing and ahing over the cute little Easter chocolate bunnies, we proceed to bite their heads off as well.

3.30 p.m.: I am back at the office and my jeans are feeling rather uncomfortable, and as much as I would like to blame the baby for this, practically speaking, if your child can walk and talk, then they have lived outside your body long enough for you to go back to your original size.

5 p.m.: I get an email from mommy dearest where she states that she has found a few of my baby pictures, and I look so cute. 'Like a giant ladoo' are her exact words.

Hmm . . . Motivation enough for me to leave the office immediately and do some sort of exercise before I become a giant ladoo all over again.

6.15 p.m.: I put my sneakers on and hit the beach for a brisk walk. I am just getting into the stride of things, listening to some great music on my iPod and enjoying the glorious view, when from the corner of my eye I see three young men creep up and, before I know it, they are passing comments, slowing down when I walk slower, quickening their steps when I try to hurry; in short, annoying the hell out of me.

This is a peculiarly Indian habit, see a woman alone anywhere and our men must harass her even if she has a moustache thicker than theirs, is eighty-three years old or has a massive mole on her nose with three strands of hair sprouting through; basically, they will revel in hounding any creature that vaguely has two X chromosomes lurking anywhere inside.

6.25 p.m.: I am now getting rather irritated with these three morons, and decide to harass them back. I make a quick U-turn and we end up face-to-face. My three true idiots also quickly turn around, so now I am following them.

I spot a large, empty coconut, pick it up and decide to throw it at their heads. They see me and start running. I am now running behind them at breakneck speed to throw my organic missile.

They are running faster and faster.
I am panting heavily and sweat
is pouring off me as I try to
chase them. Finally, one of
them trips. The other two
pull him up and drag him
away. When I finally catch up with them, I throw
the coconut, miss, and am now completely out of
breath, with a stitch on my side. I cannot chase
them further.

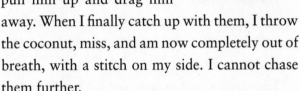

I am very frustrated as I haven't been able to
finish my walk, and my whole routine has gone
down the drain when I glance at my watch and see
that it's shockingly 6.55 p.m. I have been chasing
these morons for close to eighteen minutes. This
is the longest and fastest I have been able to run
since I was twenty-three.

I quickly calculate the calories burnt while
running behind my three idiots as compared to
my walk, and realize that I have burnt triple the
calories. Even if I had a trainer urging me to run,
I would not have been able to run at that pace for
that long and not even realize the time.

We always give our best when our back is

against the wall. We will write a superlative essay when pushing hard against a deadline, make the most innovative presentation when our job is in jeopardy, and study the hardest when the exam is the next day.

I wonder why most of us can only perform to our utmost when circumstances drive us, and then I realize that the few who push themselves are the ones who succeed.

The driven, passionate ones give their best on ordinary days and that is why they are extraordinary. As for me, I start walking back home, hoping that tomorrow I find yet another minor criminal to chase and decimate with my coconut.

I no longer have any glassware,
My carpet is threadbare,
There is a hole in the armchair,
I see a moth in my mohair,
Is this a nightmare?

H: HURRICANES HIT MY HOUSEHOLD

People inherit a lot of things from their parents. These can range from facial features to diamonds and emeralds; I have, instead, inherited a splendid member of my mother's trusted staff. His uncle works for my mother, his brother works for my grandmother, and he used to work for my aunt, but is now all mine.

Let me make it clear right at the beginning that he is the most honest, loyal person I know. I am just not sure if he is Robin to my Batman, or if he is Mogambo to my Mr India.

INCIDENT 1: It is a Sunday evening, the deadline for my weekly column is looming, and as I am sitting in front of my computer and frantically typing away, he tiptoes around me and then calls out, 'Didi! Didi!' I look up, my chain of thought all broken, and ask him what has happened. He replies, 'Do you want your shoes?'

Grr . . . For God's sake, why would I want my shoes? Does he think I can simultaneously jog on the spot while typing? I take a deep 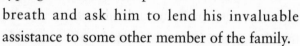 breath and ask him to lend his invaluable assistance to some other member of the family.

INCIDENT 2: I am at my neighbour's for tea when my domestic wonder calls me to say that some gentleman has entered the house and is asking for my passport, and wants to know where my computer is as well.

Rather worried, I ask my desi Jeeves if he recognizes the man, to which he replies, 'Didi, I don't think so. Looks villain type of person, come fast.'

I frantically rush home only to discover that

A: The gentleman in question is Mansukh bhai, my Internet fellow.

B: He has been asking for my laptop password, and not my passport.

I ask my domestic wonder how he can possibly not recognize Mansukh bhai who has been to the house a couple of times. He shakes his head and says, 'Mansukh bhai has a beard and this man doesn't have, also he has a big black mole on his chin. All bad people have big moles, that's why I called you.'

Wondering if it doesn't occur to him that people can perhaps shave off their beard once in a while, but not being able to wrap my brain around this evil mole bit, I have no recourse but to go to the kitchen and eat four cups of strawberry ice cream in despair.

INCIDENT 3: The bank has sent me an email saying that they have hand-delivered important papers to the house which require my signature, and need to be returned this evening.

On my arrival, I ask my Jeeves if the papers have come. He nods in the affirmative, before adding that he has kept them very safely. I ask him to fetch the papers, and go to my room to change into my trackpants. Twenty minutes later, my domestic wonder is nowhere to be seen. I search the whole house and finally spot him sitting in the staffroom, sobbing. I gently ask him what the matter is and he tells me that he had kept my papers very safely, so safely, that even he can't find them now.

I am beginning to think that he is an agent planted by L'Oréal in my house to ensure that my hair turns white overnight and thus I have to spend all my money on hair dye.

INCIDENT 4: It has been an exhausting day and all I want to do is eat some good food, and crash. I change into my pretty, pink kaftan and sit at the dining table. I have made chicken tikka, salad and mutton seekh kebab. I ask my domestic wonder to put some kebab on my plate, and he very enthusiastically scoops up two. I turn my head to see what the man of the house is trying to show me on his iPad, and plonk! I feel something on my lap. With mounting horror, I look down only to see the inevitable. There, on my lap, on my pretty, pink kaftan are two enormous pieces of kebab, two phallic-shaped massive bits of meat. I proceed to bang my head on the chair repeatedly till I calm down before asking him to lend his invaluable assistance to some other member of the family.

He will set off our alarm system repeatedly while doing mundane chores; he will knock me on the head with a cup of tea when I am sitting on my swing; he will ask me seven questions when one would be sufficient. So at the end of six months when he asks for a three-week holiday to go to his village, I am rather happy to give it to him.

Three weeks pass and he doesn't come back. The man of the house starts asking about him and accuses me of driving him away. He gives me a big lecture about how having a person with a good heart in our household is more important than having someone who will iron shirts immaculately but can never be trusted.

The man of the house is right and I am also beginning to miss my man Friday's bumbling presence in our home. I sit down to think if I have said anything to him that has made him want to leave, and feeling decidedly guilty, I call him.

He picks up and says, 'Namaste, Didi, I got on the train four days late, but now I am at Sholapur.' When I ask him why he is in Sholapur and not in Mumbai, he replies, 'Didi, I wanted to buy *shenga* chutney for you at Sholapur station, but the train was only stopping for one minute, so I pulled the alarm chain. Didi, the train people tore my shirt and made me get down, but don't worry I am reaching Mumbai very soon.'

I put the phone down, take a deep breath and immediately start doing my pranayam as I will need all the patience in the world when he finally arrives to once again lend me his invaluable assistance.

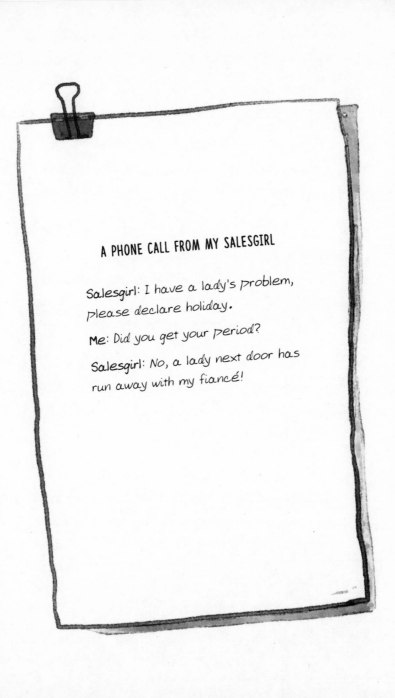

A PHONE CALL FROM MY SALESGIRL

Salesgirl: I have a lady's problem, please declare holiday.

Me: Did you get your period?

Salesgirl: No, a lady next door has run away with my fiancé!

I: I REFUSE TO CELEBRATE THIS BLOODY VALENTINE'S DAY NONSENSE

10 a.m.: It is Valentine's Day and I have informed the man of the house that it would be rather nice if he came home in the evening with a substantial gift and a bunch of white flowers. I also enlighten him with the fact that I have made a reservation at our favourite restaurant, Wasabi, for dinner at 8 p.m.

After fourteen years of matrimony, I have discovered that hoping your other half telepathically reads your mind only leads to someone wanting to punch the other one in the face.

11.15 a.m.: Trying to work from home today, I find myself sipping coffee and wasting time on Twitter, where two minutes magically stretch to twenty minutes in a second. *Interstellar*, beat that!

1.30 p.m.: My desi Jeeves walks in carrying a brown plastic bag with a few parcels neatly wrapped up in newspaper, and leaves them on my desk. I guess the man of the house has really outdone himself this year and sent presents even before his arrival.

I hastily open the packages only to find two packets of sanitary napkins and a bill for Rs 620. Apparently, the local baniya has delivered all the monthly staples today, and this is my share of the loot.

Point to be noted, milord: Why are sanitary napkins treated like radioactive isotopes? They are wrapped in layers of plastic and newspaper, then someone ties a string over this mysterious package and then it's put in a bag of its own—separate from any vegetables or cereal boxes that it may contaminate by its very presence.

Is it the fact that men will see a corner of this packet that says 'Whisper with wings', and collapse with empathy at the thought of the agony we go through every month? Or is this biological function which, in fact, enables us to give birth to specimens like them, still considered sort of unclean by mankind?

I remember a few of my school friends from conservative backgrounds telling me stories about being made to stay in isolated rooms with plates of food being left outside their door during 'that time of the month', as they were considered impure for that duration.

2 p.m.: The deadline for my *Sunday Times* column is fast approaching and since I have spent the last half hour just staring at these 'double protection, long wearing' wonders, I decide to simply write about sanitary napkins and the dreaded monthly curse, which turns out to be a bit like this:

Myths about menstruation have always been part of society and not just in India. In ancient Rome, Pliny the Elder wrote in Natural History *that dogs who tasted menstrual blood turned rabid, mares miscarried, and corn in the fields withered when menstruating women were around. In Europe, it was believed that menstruating women could spoil jam and turn wine to vinegar with their touch.*

The last nail in our coffin was provided in 1919 by Professor Schick, who cooked up the concept of 'menotoxin'. He propounded a preposterous theory that a woman's menstrual flow contains a poison, 'menotoxin', that was responsible for everything—from roses wilting to bread not rising.

Even today, menstruation is seen as dirty or unholy. My cousin once told me about having to go to a Mata ki Chowki on the same day that she got what she calls 'the monthly curse'.

Her mother protested but my cousin insisted on going along. When they reached the venue, the dupatta on the idol suddenly fell on the diya and burst into flames. My aunt caught her daughter by the ear and dragged her back home, screaming all the way that defying the period taboo had led to this calamity. My cousin's protests that a gust of wind that blew in through the open window was more likely to be the culprit was countered with another bout of religious jargon.

Well, if God disapproves of this fluid, then He should disapprove of all body fluids. So when pundits are doing yagnas and sweating copiously in front of the holy fire, shouldn't they also occasionally get burnt to a crisp by the divine cosmic forces?

Menstruating doesn't cause pickles to spoil, temples to collapse or food to rot, nor is it contagious, though it would be rather nice to infect the male population with this so-called 'curse' for a month or two, just to sit back and view what I am sure would be a highly entertaining spectacle.

At the very worst, menstruating is slightly uncomfortable, sometimes painful, and one of the most natural functions of the human body.

But we ourselves stash our sanitary napkins in secret places, are embarrassed when one falls *out of our purse by accident, and sort of tiptoe around the whole issue instead of being proud of our miraculous bodies that go on optimistically churning out eggs, month after month, for decades.*

Er . . . some of you that carry the XY chromosomes in your gene code may have found this theme rather disturbing. Could you please tuck your tail between your legs and go back to watching thirteen men running around with a bat and a ball while we decide to stop 'whispering with wings' or whispering at all, and yell and scream about this being a vital part of our biology, which, in fact, just happens to save our entire species from extinction?

5.30 p.m.: I email the piece to my editor and clamber onto my stationary bike, where I spend the next fifty minutes pedalling to nowhere, watching MTV and humming along to terrible songs about Pussy Dolls and Baby Dolls.

7 p.m.: The doorbell rings and the man of the house walks in, carrying a huge bunch of red

roses. Wondering if men are both colour-blind and deaf, I give him a sullen look and wait for my gift.

There is no gift. Apparently, he was slightly preoccupied with hanging upside down from the thirteenth floor of a building for the last six hours at the shoot and couldn't get to an Archies in time to get me a hideous, allergy-inducing furry teddy bear.

I try telling him that since I am not an eight-year-old, I was hoping for diamonds and not stuffed animals, but he interrupts and says, 'Why are you still in your dressing gown? Hurry up, or we will miss our dinner reservation!'

I sigh and say, 'I don't want to go!'

'But why?' he asks. 'Is it this teddy bear thing? I will get you one right now. The red flowers? I know, I always get you white hydrangeas but my assistant forgot and I couldn't even yell at her. She left early today saying she had some "women's troubles" or something . . . Listen, stop sulking! Get ready and let's go.'

I screech, 'It's not the flowers . . . yes it is, or maybe, I don't know, and I hate teddy bears, and I don't want to celebrate this bloody Valentine's Day nonsense, and nothing fits, my stomach is all bloated, it hurts, and I have lost my appetite.'

He smirks, 'You are not pregnant again, are you?'

'No!' I mumble. 'I just got my period and it sucks.'

I want to be a child again,
to climb up hills and roll down the
other side; only because the hill
exists and so do I.

J: JUST LEAVE ME ALONE IN JUNE

7th June: Every summer we pack up our house and throw everything we can find in massive suitcases and head off on our annual vacation.

This year we have three extra bags that carry all the essential requirements of a very tiny person: The baby. How can an 11-kilo baby need 85 kilos of things is a calculation that would involve equations of relativity that I can't solve. All I can do is make lists and go on packing.

I desperately call my mother, asking for her

help. She arrives in half an hour, and instead of assisting me with the mundane task of organizing diapers and matching hairbands, decides that all the paintings in my house have to be rearranged at this very moment.

I am standing helplessly in the midst of six suitcases and she has badgered my staff to drop everything they were doing, including last-minute washing and ironing, and they are now all busy drilling holes in my walls.

8th June: We are at the airport and what was supposed to be a smooth journey has now descended into utter pandemonium. The man of the house has decided that he wants to fly in a particular airline only—so a trip that should

have taken us around five hours has become a mammoth ten-hour journey.

I decide not to grumble about the delay that this will cause us and quietly board the flight.

An hour later, as I am about to fall asleep, I spot a fellow passenger who is also from showbiz and who happens to be mommy dearest's colleague. He guzzles down (what is probably) his fifth whisky and then gets up to go to the galley to scrounge around for his next drink. Having accomplished his mission, he comes back and sits down, only to have the stewardess run towards him and pull him off his seat violently.

Our friend was so inebriated that he could barely see and had actually perched himself ON TOP of a frail old woman asleep in her own seat. Blimey!

We have reached Dubai where we have a three-hour halt. Our son is an excellent mimic but performing little acts like pretending to be a British old lady looking for cinnamon buns or a teenage Chinese pop star, in the middle of Dubai's international airport can cause him to be deported; as I am desperately looking for a burka to gag him with, the baby decides she must go to the bathroom right then, but will not sit without her pink Hello Kitty potty seat.

We are aimlessly sitting at the lounge. The man of the house is looking at his iPad, our son is dozing off on the couch and the baby is on my shoulder. I am singing a song to her which has something to do with the moon, but since it is made up by me and not Gulzar, it consists of only two words: *Chanda* and *aaja*.

I am finally at peace and she is giving me a tight hug. This is what makes it all worthwhile, this tiny moment of joy when suddenly I yelp—the little beast has nipped me hard on my arm and is grinning, saying, 'I doing biting.'

Why did I have these children? If I merely wanted to be tortured, I could have just gotten weekly tattoos rather than have voluntarily reproduced these tiny 'mini-mes' albeit with martial-art skills.

I vaguely remember travelling with my parents when I was a little girl. Did my mom also run behind us like this? Did she not want to be free sometimes, just to breathe, with no one tugging her shirt, no one asking her what's for dinner? Free to fly wherever she wanted, do whatever she wanted, whenever she wanted. Life is full of contradictions. We crave security and independence in equal measures.

As I am in the midst of my random musings, my reverie is interrupted by the man of the house saying, 'I am hungry, let's get some food!'

Sometimes I am glad I am not a philosopher— how would I ever complete a single chain of thought when someone is constantly asking me to do something? I don't think Plato would have been able to write his dialogues if he had a wife who kept bugging him to pass the pita bread.

9th June: Our holiday has officially begun and I am relishing the prospect of idling away my days. This is the time I switch off, work on my tan, and leave carpenters, cement dust and wax fumes behind.

An hour later, I am still sitting on my bed, sipping coffee and enjoying the idea of doing absolutely nothing, when my son barges in and declares that I have to go 'zip lining' with him.

Technically, 'zip lining' is riding a wire that is tied between two distant points very high up in the air. You get into a harness, send a prayer up to whatever God you believe in, let go, and hope that you will reach the other end in one piece.

I put away all thoughts of lazing on the beach, reading a new book about spaceships and aliens on my iPad, and decide to give Mother India some stiff competition in sacrificing my needs before the needs of my offspring.

Sweating in the blistering heat and sitting in a boat for forty minutes, we finally reach the island where we are supposed to participate in this strange sport. I am ready in my harness and, as I start, I realize that this is not just plain zip lining that I have been cornered into doing—it's zip lining with an aerial obstacle course.

The next hour passes with me crawling through nets, trying to walk on a balance beam and doing splits to go from one moving step to another; all the while trying not to look down because I am 40 feet above the ground.

Every muscle in my body is sore. I hurt my wrist last week and all this climbing and crawling is really causing it to flare up. All I want to do is give up, when my son, who is merrily crossing each hurdle, calls out, 'Mom, why are you moving so slowly? Are you already tired?'

I want to yell at him for putting me through this; yell at him for not realizing that I am not eleven like him, or twenty-one or even thirty-one any more.

I don't say a word because children are always learning from us. They don't pay attention to most of the stuff we say, but are always watching what we do. Do I really want him to see that when life gets even remotely challenging, one must complain, crib and quit? I strengthen my resolve, plaster a cheerful smile and finish the obstacle course.

The ordeal is over and when I am finally climbing down the exit ladder, I realize that I am exhausted and exhilarated at the same time. I feel truly alive because I have been living in the moment, hurdle to hurdle, with no time or energy to think about anything else.

We grown-ups always try to take the easy way out, the laziest way. We seem to have a great fear of getting tired, as if any energy depleted is lost forever. We want to plan our fatigue the same way we plan everything else. Most of us barely move till we have that one hour in the gym that we have decided we should expend physical energy on. And there, too, we time ourselves, count the precise repetitions we need to do, adjust our speed to what the heart-rate monitor indicates we should move at and go on practising our robotic routines day in and day out.

I wish we lived like children. Run till you are out of breath, flop on the grass, stare at clouds, jump up again, chase a squirrel around every tree in the park, walk on your hands because the world looks different upside down, climb little hills and roll down the other side, do somersaults . . . just because you can.

What do we do instead? We surround ourselves with all these big and small blinking screens, while our bodies and minds slowly forget how to tumble, how to wonder, how to live.

THREE MAGICAL INDIAN THINGS

1. Magical godmen: Currently most are not actively practising as they are fighting various rape/scam cases, but they will soon be out on bail and create flowers out of water, help you beget a child, and manifest sindoor out of thin air. But ladies, please maintain a physical gap of minimum six feet—safely out of lunging distance.

2. Magical black thread: An ebony thread around ankles and wrists; when people think foul thoughts about you, the miracle thread violently repels them. I have been trying to sell yards of it to the Pentagon but surprisingly, no luck yet. (Honest confession—my children, too, have one firmly wrapped around their wrist!)

3. Magic rings: Yellow sapphire on the first finger, an emerald on the little one . . . all for prosperity. There's even a cure for piles—just wear an iron ring on the correct finger (take that, you silly ones, who slogged in medical school for years!).

K: KARAN JOHAR CELEBRATES
KARVA CHAUTH

6 p.m.: Am I curled up on my couch reading *Harry Potter and the Goblet of Fire*? Am I getting ready for an infamous Bollywood party or am I sitting in a salwar kameez getting henna applied on my palms in preparation for tomorrow's torturous fast? No prizes for guessing this one. I am one of the many fortunate women who get to stay hungry and thirsty all day in order to magically lengthen my other half's life.

In ancient times, I can appreciate why one would enthusiastically undertake such a task—if you know that as soon as your other half pops it, someone is going to make you jump into a large, blazing fire and commit sati. I can completely understand the motivation to try any means to prolong your husband's lifespan, but today, when the unfortunate circumstance of your spouse's demise merely frees you up to place ads in the matrimonial column, go on online dating sites and feverishly attend bar nights, the zeal for such taxing endeavours seems a bit extreme . . .

5 a.m.: If there is a God, He hates me. I can't think of any other reason why I am stumbling around the house at this unearthly hour normally reserved for owls, bats and the man of the house.

5.30 a.m.: My mother-in-law has sent me a big basket of fruits and sweets which I must eat before sunrise so that I can starve the entire day, thereby triggering a mystical spell (known only to Indians and NRI fans of Karan Johar movies) that will enable her beloved son to live a long life. I have tried to protest that the newspaper states sunrise is at 6.31 a.m., so I could technically wake up at 6.15 a.m. and gulp some food before the crucial moment the above-mentioned spell loses power, but to no avail.

When I further point out that the pet tortoise in our garden is definitely going to outlive all of us and I don't see anyone fasting for him, I get a withering look from her and a sharp nudge in the ribs from the man of the house.

10 a.m.: I gulp my saliva since that is the only liquid I am allowed to consume, and call a fellow member of the Karva Chauth Torture Club who goes on to tell me how lucky I am because she has to follow stricter rules than me. She is not allowed to wash her hair on Karva Chauth. She chuckles that even if a crow shits on her head today, she will still have to walk around with it because all her mother-in-law will tell her is that it is inauspicious to wet her hair today, but will not find it inauspicious to have a daughter-in-law who smells of crap.

11 a.m.: I need water . . .

1 p.m.: I need coffee . . .

3 p.m.: I need water, coffee and a large Scotch on the rocks . . .

4 p.m.: I know that all our Indian customs are based on scientific research by ancient minds where they spent decades examining and experimenting before they came up with specific rituals to ensure our well-being; so I do my own scientific research (which takes me a little less than five minutes, via Google) and the results are unmistakable. The United Nations research states that men with the longest life expectancy are from Japan, followed by Switzerland. I am rather surprised at this result as since time immemorial we have been doing the Karva Chauth fast to make sure our men have long lives, and the results should have definitely shown by now.

I scan the list, confident that in this chart of life expectancy, the Indian man must definitely be in the top 5. Nope! There are 146 countries above us where the men have longer lifespans, and the biggest blow is that even with four wives who don't fast for them, the Arab men outlive our good old Indian dudes.

6 p.m.: We Indians are a strange race; we send MOM to Mars, but listen to mom-in-law and look for the moon. One of the better qualities we possess is that most of us will follow traditions and rituals as long as they do not demean or harm us, or cause us to do the same to another, while making our elders happy. We simply do it rather than prove a point as to how liberated and independent we truly are. Perhaps, this is how we harmoniously hold our large families together as we celebrate different aspects of our lives.

9 p.m.: Dressed in our finery, we gather on a friend's terrace to look for the moon. As banal as I find most rituals, I am still swept away by the moment. A dark night, five good friends, sparkling with our bindis, zardozi and red outfits. We are giggling and taking pictures. Suddenly, someone spots the hazy orange outline of the moon, and

we are now dragging out our men, laughing as we
borrow things from each other's plates, a strainer,
a coconut barfi, a flower, laughing as we borrow
things from our past . . .

Let me count the ways I love you . . .
It's a lot more than just two.

L: LOVE IS IMPERFECTLY PERFECT

6.30 a.m.: I am trying to wake our son up and he moans that he isn't feeling well, and doesn't want to go to school. I yank his blanket off and then realize that he is shivering.

I need to take his temperature, and after rummaging through various first-aid kits that we keep in the house, I find three thermometers. One doesn't beep even if you keep it in your mouth for twenty minutes, the second has so many buttons that you may need to get in touch with the call centre for technical help, and the third one shows the temperature, but only in Celsius. My capacity for mentally converting this into our good old Indian Fahrenheit is severely limited. Hmm . . . Internet to the rescue.

10 a.m.: I finally get hold of the doctor on the phone and he says that it is probably some viral bug, and prescribes a few medicines.

10.30 a.m.: We are now tucked into my bed and the son decides he doesn't 'do' medicines and will let his body heal naturally. I can sense the influence of a certain well-built gentleman who drinks yucky vegetable juices and also doesn't 'do' medicines.

11 a.m.: I have decided to stay home today so that I can keep an eye on our son, cuddle up with him and watch horror movies. We start with *The Ring*.

11.03 a.m.: The first scary bit comes on and our son screams. Movie frantically paused. My horror movie plan has been declared a big flop, and the man of the house has fired me (after our self-righteous son called him up and gleefully informed him of the above proceedings), saying I am frying our son's brains further by showing him ghosts and blood.

3 p.m.: I have now bought a Vicks thermometer (no, I am not their brand ambassador or any such thing). It is the fastest, most amazing device, and thankfully gives the temperature in useful Fahrenheit. I love it so much that I feel like carrying it in my bag and randomly taking people's temperatures with it. Well, for now, I make myself happy by just taking mine.

8 p.m.: The man of the house is home and is very grumpy because he feels there isn't enough food (enough food for whom? An army? Ludhiana? Thirty-eight hungry boy scouts?). Punjabis are very fussy about their food. If there are only four

dishes on the table, then they either feel: a) Very humiliated or b) Miss their mother. I am not yet sure which one is worse.

1.30 a.m.: Our son wakes up saying he is feeling very cold and can I turn the AC down. As I am fumbling in my sleep with the remote, the man of the house shouts that our son is burning up.

Temperature quickly checked with the amazing thermometer and it shows 104 degrees. I throw Calpol down his throat, and the man of the house decides to sponge him with cold water.

I keep insisting that he leave it to me as he has an early shoot tomorrow, but he doesn't stop, tells me to go to sleep, and continues the cold compress.

As my eyes are shutting, I think about the word 'love'. It is multilayered, convoluted and as imperfect as all human emotions. It is not your heart beating fast when you look at him (I even knew a girl who would throw up each time she saw her beloved) or constantly wanting to be with the other person. Love in any relationship, family or an intimate friendship, is only about putting the other person's needs ahead of your own, and that, my friend, is just as simple and as complex as you make it.

FOUR WAYS TO DEAL WITH SNORING

1. Get your pepper shaker and gently sprinkle some pepper around his nasal passage. A violent sneezing fit may open up some congestion and allow you a few hours of calm dreamtime.

2. Practise meditation in order to ignore disturbances. Inhale slowly. Exhale slowly. Now just repeat the same sequence 28,800 times.

3. Carry your spouse to the garden, throw him in the fish pond and then convince him in the morning that he has also started sleepwalking.

4. Article 463 of the Indian Constitution gives you the right to smother him with a pillow.

Disclaimer: Some of these methods may work, some may not and some will send you straight to jail or worse. Please use the above suggestions at your own discretion.

M: MASKED BANDIT ON THE PROWL

SATURDAY

4 a.m.: I am wide awake and it's not because of the sonorous snores of the man of the house, but because I am in the midst of a full-blown panic attack. In precisely three hours, I have to magically transform from a middle-aged, vaguely stylish woman, to an ageless goddess.

6.15 a.m.: Standing in front of our hallway mirror, I am practising a few poses, one leg artfully bent, the opposite shoulder up, when the man of the house strides in and decides to share: a) I look like I have dislocated my shoulder; and b) Has anyone ever told me I strongly resemble Tom Cruise? I am not sure at this point if he is trying to say that I look like a short man or just stating that I have major movie-star-like charisma, so I silently let it pass.

10 a.m.: I am ready with make-up and not a hair out of place at the photo shoot for a fashion magazine in a shiny pink dress with massive pearls all around the hem. It's a stunning outfit, but every time I want to sit, these pearls dig into my bottom. I resolve to remain standing till the next outfit change . . . before these pearls have a chance to follow the famous *Star Trek* slogan 'to boldly go where no man has gone before'. Yikes!

11 a.m.: My baby is here. I rush to hug her before I go for my next shot where I am leaning on a fairy-tale dwarf, and this particular dwarf is insisting on talking to me in Marathi, which I really can't understand. I wonder if Snow White had similar

communication problems with her bunch of men.

11.45 a.m.: Glittering in an all-gold Pucci dress and boiling in Maharashtra's scorching sun, I am perched on a carriage. My body, of its own accord, dredges up some rusty skills, and soon I am pouting and preening like this is my daily job.

1.30 p.m.: The next change is a black Cavalli dress with a plunging neckline. As I tug it over my head, I realize there is no way I can wear anything inside.

1.40 p.m.: I am now walking to my next location and the only thing keeping my breasts in place is hope!

2.30 p.m.: The shoot has come to an end and I have finally figured out why 90 per cent of women on the red carpet (and in magazines) pose like a teapot, with their hands on their waist—it makes you look a lot thinner.

As I make a mental note to go everywhere with my hands perched on my midsection, I begin to wonder will I truly look wonderfully lean or will I be giving people the idea that I have a bad stomach ache?

7.15 p.m.: I want to do something simple tonight, and when our son suggests that we go to the cinema with the family, I am more than happy.

8.30 p.m.: I walk out of the house having hurriedly thrown on my blue worn-out kurta; am carrying a bright yellow bag (which clashes terribly but I am too lazy to change it) and not a slick of make-up.

8.45 p.m.: Hmm . . . The kids are eating Bavarian chocolate ice cream, and tired of being deprived, I, too, have one. My niece is eating a chicken burger, so I have one, and the man of the house orders some bhel, so I have some too.

This is almost more food than I have consumed in the last two weeks, but I think sometimes you have to eat till you burst, the same way that you need to laugh till tears roll down your face.

10.30 p.m.: The movie is over and all I want to do is fall on my bed and hope I am able to digest a quarter of what I have eaten. The man of the house walks me to the elevator and then suddenly decides that he would rather run down the five floors. I can't seem to see the rest of the family, so I take the lift down humming some tuneless song. I walk out to the car only to almost fall down as a dozen flashbulbs go off in my face.

For anyone who has ever thought that these encounters with the paparazzi are pre-planned, kindly use some common sense. We have some sort of vanity as well and allowing yourself to be photographed in a state that you would not want to put up on Facebook, let alone be published in national newspapers, would be rather demented.

10.45 p.m.: I reach home only to find the man of the house perched on the sofa, as he had quickly escaped on his bulldozer bodyguard's bike, leaving me to face the music. I box him on the head, sulk and go to bed.

SUNDAY

I had promised our son that I would take him to see *Lucy*, and being a sci-fi fan myself, I am also excited to watch it, though it means a visit to the cinema again, but I have decided that the press is not going to catch me off guard again. I blow-dry my hair, wear a cute top, and a pair of extremely uncomfortable heels. I reach the theatre with my best smile, and wouldn't you know it, there is not a camera in sight!

Getting rather fed up of not knowing when to be picture-perfect ready or slouch in my trackpants, I have come up with a great plan.

I print out a 12-inch picture of Mr Modi's face, make two holes on the side, string it, and voila, I am now prepared to go to the cinema. Each time I go to the movies, I will just pull out my home-made Mr Modi mask and simply put it on.

THE PROS:

1) I do not have to put any make-up on ever again.

2) I will prove that I am a loyal, patriotic Indian citizen.

3) I may become a nationwide trendsetter.

THE CONS:

1) Terrorists might get confused thinking I am the prime minister and attempt to assassinate me.
2) The government may think it is a great idea and make wearing these masks mandatory.
3) A fairness cream brand may decide to cash in on MY trend and develop an anti-ageing SPF 30 (patent pending) Mr Modi mask that makes your skin lighter with every wear, and not give me a penny.

By the way, if you do go to the movies this week and spot our prime minister, looking remarkably slimmer, casually slipping out of the theatre in a faded blue kurta and a bright yellow bag, don't get foxed, it's probably just me.

TWO KINDS OF PEOPLE YOU MEET
ON A PLANE

1. The talker: This is the one who happens to sit next to you and then talks to you for the entire eight-hour journey. Just because someone is strapped to their seat and is a captive audience, don't drive them to a point where they try to depressurize the cabin by digging a hole in the window with their tweezers and praying for the oxygen mask to drop down just to stop the sound of your voice!

2. The nitpicker: This is the traveller who's upset about everything. He will rudely demand to meet the captain to check on the delay, will send back his meal as it's unappetizing, and will complain about the crying baby six rows behind—does he really think that the harassed-looking mother is purposely pinching her child to make him cry?

N: NOT QUITE A FEMINIST, SO HOW DID I REACH MARS?

WEDNESDAY

7 a.m.: I am in a plane heading to Delhi for an export trade fair. Have you ever been inside a closed space, early in the morning, with people who have apparently eaten chicken makhani and *aloo gobi* the previous night, have rushed to the airport in the morning and then decided

to immerse their fellow passengers in aromatic fumes?

Why does the oxygen mask only come down in emergencies? And if this is not an emergency, then what is?

TO-DO LIST

1. Get off flight and dry-clean pashmina shawl, yellow T-shirt, J Brand jeans, grey bag, watch, ring and mobile.

2. Shake hair vigorously to loosen out embedded smell before corporate meeting.

3. Write to the government not to waste funds on nuclear warheads, can reroute the same plane to an enemy country. If the government can provide a single matchstick, then the gaseous plane will explode in beautiful flames.

7.15 a.m.: The plane is taxiing and fellow political passenger behind my seat is shouting into his mobile phone, 'How will the prosperity come in the India? You tell me, yah! Yadav is best in the

India and how you put the lime to turn milk into the curd, so we have put him to turn the party.'

7.19 a.m.: The plane has taken off and fellow passenger is still shouting, 'Arrey, he is not milk-drinking child, *wo toh saap hai saap*' (a reptilian mammal—interesting). After a while, silence . . . Either he finally lost signal or someone discreetly stabbed him. Either way, all's well that ends well.

THURSDAY

11 a.m.: I am sitting and eating chips at my little candle booth at the trade fair. A working woman's constant companion is guilt. We are always feeling the burden of periodically neglecting either our children or our work. Today is my son's parent–teacher meeting and instead of being at school, I have to be here, listening to nonsense like, 'My real cousin brother is going to foreign,' 'What is your good name?' And 'I myself Mr Lokesh.'

12.30 p.m.: Three new customers introduce themselves to me, saying, 'I am Kapil the elder brother' and 'I am Sonu the younger brother', and the third one chirps in, 'I am Pradeep the medium-sized brother.' Hmm . . . Nice to know that all good things come in medium size.

I ask them if there are any other brothers, and they sadly say that there was a fourth but in childhood, '*Wo off ho gaya*' (not quite sure if they were talking about their brother or a light bulb that went off). I commiserate with them and after taking down their orders, I bid them adieu.

During the afternoon lull, I pull out my phone to check my messages. After the parent–teacher meeting yesterday, a whole bunch of moms are having a heated discussion on our class WhatsApp group chat. Suddenly, an irate father comes onto the chat, rants a bit, and then says, 'Some things may be above the control of the moms, so we should make a father's group to tackle it.' There is pindrop silence on the chat. I am sure this poor chap couldn't possibly mean this the way it sounds. It would be suicidal to say this on a group chat dominated by school moms, because you may find it is totally within these women's control to wait for you on the school steps, hoist you above their shoulders and throw you in the nearest garbage bin.

3.30 p.m.: Needing a break, I start walking around the trade fair. I pause to look at some goblets and trays displayed at a booth, when the owner comes up to me and says, 'You also got the same phone, ah? Me too, yaa. Same to same, what's your sweet name?'

Restraining myself from violently throwing up on him, I smile and say, 'My name is Khan and I am not a terrorist.'

Let him go figure that one out.

4.18 p.m.: Sign on the next booth says, 'Entry from backside only!' I think I will just skip this one and return to my candle booth.

FRIDAY

My Noida trip has come to an end, and armed with a few large orders and having learnt new phrases like, 'If you can do, do, if cannot, then admit yourself', I decide to get home quickly before I need to admit myself to a mental asylum.

SATURDAY

My gynaecologist has asked me to attend a conference on women's empowerment at the Ambani hospital. This is the same man who has pulled two children out of me and can confidently say that he literally knows me inside out. I often make (not very funny) jokes that his idea of foreplay is perhaps tapping his wife on the head, as that is the one bit he must not be seeing the entire day.

My name is called out and I get onto the stage; my heart is beating fast and my legs are a bit shaky, but speak I must, so this is what I say.

'Our little satellite reached Mars because it was called MOM. If it was called DAD, it would still be circling the Earth, lost, but not willing to ask for directions.

'In order to empower women, we need three things: education, employment and a change in the way men perceive women.

'How do we change this deeply ingrained perception? We are mothers. We are the ones raising an entire new generation. We shape their values and attitudes. We need to teach them right from the beginning that both genders are different, but our value is the same. If we want to empower women, we need to be empowered mothers so that we can lead the next generation of men and women into a life of true equality.'

That evening, I ask the man of the house, 'So do you think we are equals or am I weaker in any way?' He laughs, 'Of course, you are weaker!' And trying to imitate me, in a ridiculous falsetto voice, continues, 'Baby, push this coffee table, na, I can't move it.'

I mutter under my breath that I wasn't talking about physical strength, punch him on the arm and go off to see what's made for dinner, check on our son's homework and send two emails, while the man of the house keeps circling around the television and the couch.

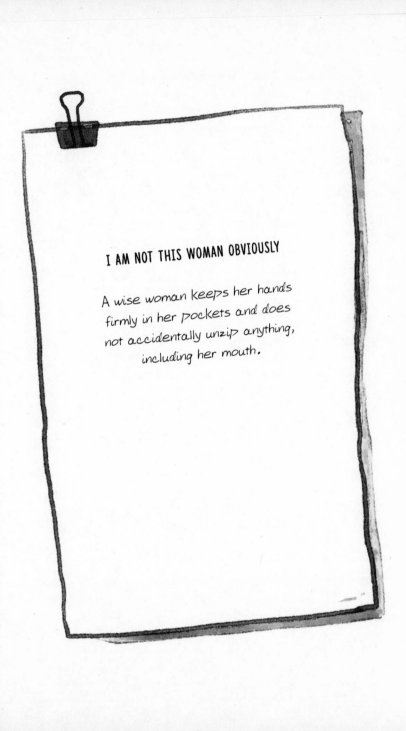

I AM NOT THIS WOMAN OBVIOUSLY

A wise woman keeps her hands
firmly in her pockets and does
not accidentally unzip anything,
including her mouth.

O: OH NO! I AM UNDER ARREST!

The man of the house is the showstopper at a fashion show for a denim brand and is also the star of their advertising campaign called Unbutton.

I go along to see the show and am sitting in the front row. The show starts and in the bright glare of a single spotlight the Mister walks down the ramp, stands in front of me and tells me to open the top button of his jeans—all this as part of the advertising gimmick.

I am horrified and keep shaking my head, but he takes my hands up to his waist and I quickly open a single top button in the manner of a harried mother opening her toddler's pants.

The next morning my husband is getting awarded the Padma Shri, one of the highest awards given to civilians in India. We are at the award ceremony and I am grinning, posing in a group picture with the President of India when my phone pings, and I see a message from my mom: 'The police are looking for you, some crazy activist has filed a case and now they want to arrest you for indecent behaviour.' Arghh! How can this happen to me? If nothing else, can't they wait till I finish taking a selfie with the President?

Two days later, I am sitting at the police station where they are taking my fingerprints and asking me if I have any identifying scars. Yes, identifying scars! Like I get into regular knife fights and get grazed by bullets.

They won't arrest scores of men who publicly unbutton, unzip, pull out their dangly bits and proceed to urinate on a wall right outside the police station, but for reasons still unknown to me, opening a single top button has become the crime of the century.

In order to finally come home to my kids, I pay a bail amount of Rs 500 and have my mug shot framed on the wall of Juhu police station right beside other notorious people like Moti Munni (who runs an escort service) and Mallika Sherawat who does not.

Final tally of this little adventure?

The man of the house has a big fat cheque from the denim company and he also has the Padma Shri, while I have the privilege of carving out my place in the history books by taking part in an obscene crime. Blimey!

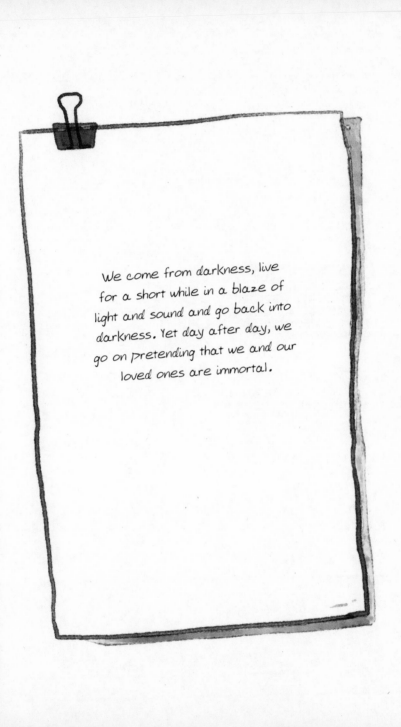

We come from darkness, live
for a short while in a blaze of
light and sound and go back into
darkness. Yet day after day, we
go on pretending that we and our
loved ones are immortal.

P: PLEASE DON'T LET GO

10 a.m.: I'm enjoying Sunday breakfast with the whole family. My in-laws always put enough food on the table to feed half of Amritsar. We're digging into aloo parathas with home-made ghee, and as I am despairing at the horrific number of calories being consumed, the phone rings and we get some terrible news. A family friend has lost her young son. The young man, in his early twenties, went to America to attend a friend's wedding, left a suicide note on Facebook and

killed himself before anyone could reach him.

I cannot even begin to imagine what his mother is going through. There is no pain greater than losing a child. From the time they are in your stomach; from hearing their heartbeats on the sonogram and counting kicks in your last trimester—you begin your journey of worry. You worry about their health, their education, their career, their spouses, their children. Worrying, but not really believing that one unlucky day your greatest fear may actually come true.

You lose a child to an accident or an illness, and with a broken heart, you console yourself that you did your best, it's perhaps God's will, he has gone to a better place; but when your child decides that the life he has been given, the life where everything he knows is what you have taught him, is not worth living, how do you live with that? How do you stop blaming yourself? How do you go on?

JODHPUR: A girl studying in the ninth grade hanged herself from a fan after being regularly teased by a boy at school.

BANGALORE: Two teenagers committed suicide by jumping into a water tank after being fired by their teacher for their poor academic performance.

MUMBAI: A fourteen-year-old girl hanged herself because she was harassed by her neighbour.

CHANDIGARH: A twenty-one-year-old student jumped to her death from the sixth floor of her hostel, leaving a note that included wishing her sisters success in every field.

KOLKATA: Two teenage girls committed suicide in a village near Kolkata, disillusioned about their future as a same-sex couple.

We teach our children to study hard, to strive to succeed, but do we teach them that it's okay to fail? That life is about accepting yourself? That there is no stigma in seeking help? Our Indian culture is based on worshipping our parents. We grow up listening to words like 'respect', 'obedience' and 'tradition'. Can we not add the words 'communication', 'unconditional love' and 'support' to this list?

I look at the WHO research. The highest rate of suicide in India is among the age group of fifteen to twenty-nine. Do we even talk to our teens about this?

2 p.m.: We normally spend our Sundays by the poolside or going to the cinema, but today we just get a few groceries and spend time quietly in our kitchen, putting a small meal together.

6.30 p.m.: I am standing in the balcony, sipping some coffee and looking at the sunset. The children have taken the dogs and gone down to play on the beach. I spot my son. He is standing on the sand, right at the edge of the ocean, flying a blue kite.

The kite goes high and then swings low till it almost seems to fall into the water, and all I want to say to him is that soon he will see that life is just like flying a kite. Sometimes you have to leave it loose, sometimes you have to hold on tight, sometimes your kite will fly effortlessly, sometimes you will not be able to control it, but even when you are struggling to keep it afloat and the string is cutting into your fingers, don't let go.

The wind will change in your favour once again, my son. Just don't let go . . .

The prodigal son has been informing every guest that comes to our house: 'Mom says she hates festivals, wants to drink beer, ride her yellow scooter and run over random people who burst crackers.'

For the record:
1) Yes, I partially said that and my son is an annoying eavesdropper.
2) I was joking.
3) I don't drink anything that's the colour of discarded body fluids.
4) I have no plans to run over anyone because I, too, will fall off my scooter! (Point to be noted, milord.)

Q: QUARTER OF A CENTURY AGO

1990

8.30 a.m.: Goa. The minute you land, you feel free. It's the wonderful bracing air, and with all the leftover wafts of weed in circulation, a sense of well-being is pretty much guaranteed I reckon.

1 p.m.: We are at this little café called Orange Boom. I am stuffing my mouth with avocado–mushroom toast, and sprawled beside me are my

dear friend (who we shall call Miss D) and the four boys that form our group.

Isn't it strange that there will always be one moment you will recall when someone asks you when were you the happiest? For me, it has always been this day. Somewhere this tiny, seemingly unimportant day wedged itself so firmly into my heart that decades later, I will find myself bringing the man of the house and my children to this café again and again.

I will buy a blue house just around the corner and I will get a yellow scooter of my own, almost identical to the one I am just about learning to ride now.

But at this point, I don't know any of this and the only thing on my mind is learning to ride this bloody scooter. Relying on the boys for rides to parties is a risky proposition. We always want to leave early and they sometimes want to stay back till the sun comes up and sets all over again.

2.30 p.m.: The boys have gone ahead and we have taken a tiny detour to pick up our beach essentials before joining them. Zipping along on my yellow scooter with Miss D sitting behind me, I suddenly realize that my silver ring is slipping out of my finger. I look down to quickly push it back on and my scooty hits a pothole, and Miss D and me are now flying through the air, only to land in a straw-filled ditch on the side of the road.

2.35 p.m.: We are hanging out in a ditch at the side of the road, strangely in the same position as we were sitting on the scooter, though the bike is bent in a weird way. We enlist the help of passing ravers and druggies (very kind people when they are not going through any manic withdrawal symptoms) to get us out of our shallow hole and set us on our way.

3.35 p.m.: We have finally reached the beach shack. Our friends are looking suspiciously at us and the first question is, 'Did you fall somewhere?' We firmly deny such outrageous accusations; then they say, 'Why is there straw in your hair? And the scooter also looks crooked.' They finally buy all our denials and leave us alone. We are now surreptitiously putting cold beer cans on our bruises and only limping when the boys are preoccupied with the volleyball-playing bikini-clad bombshells on the beach.

6.30 p.m.: Riding my yellow scooter back to our rented cottage, with the wind blowing through my hair and an orange and purple sunset setting the sky ablaze, my perfect day is almost over; only to do everything again the next day and the next, for as many days as the whim strikes us.

2014

Miss D and I are now grown women. We have amassed four children, two husbands and three dogs between the two of us, and over coffee we start talking about our old group, reminiscing about our past escapades and adventures with the boys and then we realize that none of these boys (now middle-aged men) are married.

Just for the record, these are all straight, financially solvent men; so to unravel their mysterious bachelorhood and to thoroughly entertain ourselves in the bargain, we decide to

don our Sherlock and Dr Watson
hats and investigate the matter.

Whipping out our phones and
putting them on speaker mode,
we start our unrehearsed phone
questionnaires, which go a bit like
this . . .

Me: 'Hey, what's up? A quick question
and then you can go back to dealing with the
Municipal Corporation of Greater Mumbai: Why
are you not married?'

Bachelor No. 1: 'Are you nuts? You forgot I
am divorced? None of you liked my wife, kept
complaining that she smells of methi.'

I hastily disconnect the phone and call the next
candidate on our list.

Me: 'Hi! Quick question, why have you never
been married?'

Bachelor: 'Oh God! I think you have pressed
redial because I have already given you that
answer, now can I go back to earning a living?'

Oops . . .

We eat a few more chocolate biscuits, and my willing accomplice calls the next candidate.

She: 'Hey, buddy! Wanted to ask, why are you still single?'

Bachelor No. 2: 'Baby, suddenly fancy me after all these years?'

She: 'Shut up! I am doing a survey, dude.'

Bachelor No. 2: '*Gussa ho gai!* Your fault for asking such questions at this hour.'

She: 'It's 11 a.m., you idiot!'

Bachelor No. 2: 'Oh! I am at a three-day rave in Goa, baby, lost track of time.'

Phone disconnected.

My turn again, and from the other end, a raspy voice answers, 'I have already got a message about the daft survey you psychos are doing and I don't want to be part of it . . .' And he continues in his peculiarly self-important manner, 'By the way, mummy forgot to send tandoori chicken today and my fund manager is coming over, so it's good you girls called. Can you send a tiffin over please and send some gulab jamuns; my girlfriend is also coming, so send food for three–four people.' As he pauses, I quickly interject, 'Oh, your relationship with the seventeen-year-old must be going really well since . . .' He screeches, 'I am sick of telling you she is twenty-four!' And hangs up.

The last man standing is now on the phone . . .

Me: 'We are conducting an investigation. Can you please tell us, why haven't you ever been married?'

Bachelor No. 4: 'Has my mother put you guys up to this? I don't want to talk about it.'

We persist till he finally tells us his story.

He was dating a Gujarati girl and one day in the grip of passion and wanting to emulate the West in this act, along with everything else, started spanking his girlfriend on the bottom, while saying, 'Who's your daddy? Who's your daddy?'

The Gujarati girl, who I assume had never played this particular game before, called out shrilly, 'Hasmukh Patel! Hasmukh Patel is my daddy!'

Unfortunately, my friend's name is not Hasmukh Patel.

After that, each time he saw her in the buff, he would visualize her father: the pudgy, bespectacled Mr Hasmukh Patel and, in despair, had no recourse but to terminate their alliance. He has never been able to find the right girl since.

He sorrowfully recounts this story, and we commiserate with him till he bursts out laughing, and we realize that we have just been bamboozled.

These men have no tragic stories about losing the one that mattered, but are incredibly happy without what they see as the shackles of matrimony. While we feel sorry for them and worry about what they will do as they get older, they, in fact, feel sorry for us, as they see our lives as endless piles of diapers and suffocating predictability. Case closed, Dr Watson.

We put the phone down and though our lives are filled with all sorts of fulfilling things, talking to our old group again leads to a certain kind of wistfulness.

This is perhaps what middle age truly is—the future we dreamed about is a place that we now firmly inhabit, so we spend a little more time looking over our shoulder at the beguiling sepia-coloured postcards from our past where we once stood before an esoteric world of myriad prospects and were mesmerized at the possibilities it held . . .

Don't look down on people
because then they can see the
crap stuck up your nostril.

R: REACHING FOR THE VOMIT BAG

The man of the house has summoned the entire family to Delhi where he has his next shoot. The prodigal son has a broken foot, the baby has a cough and I am down with a bout of insurmountable inertia—a strange malady that renders the sufferer incapable of making to-do lists, let alone pack 400 miscellaneous items that may never be needed.

I have had a very tough week and all I want to do is get into my bed, read sci-fi short stories and drink hot chocolate, but the new-age Indian woman's work is never done because she has to do all the stuff that was dumped on men earlier, like dealing with doctors, talking to bankers, bribing random government officials, threatening accountants, and still has to change diapers, tolerate crazy mothers-in-law and jump at her family's commands.

So when our son jabs me with his crutches and demands to know when we are leaving, I sigh deeply and simply do the needful.

THE PLANE RIDE: I am getting into the plane and I push all my eleven carry-on pieces, of differing sizes, including the above-mentioned crutches into various compartments, and settle into my seat only to find that my fellow passenger is another woman roughly my age, travelling with her husband, and a baby on her lap. Looking forward to exchanging stories and tips on babies and motherhood, I settle my limping warrior into his seat, plonk my baby on my lap and buckle up for the ride.

The plane takes off and my baby starts yelling.

I am trying to make her drink water so that her ears pop open. The baby starts chewing the in-flight magazine, the same magazine handled by hordes of people who may not all wash their hands after using the airplane toilet. I snatch it from her and console myself that perhaps the baby will have a stronger immune system because of this continuous exposure to germs.

The baby is now trying to bite the seatbelt, trying to bite my yellow handbag, hitting me on the nose with her genetically made-for-karate hands—generally making my life hell, as usual. The woman in the next seat who is still calmly holding her sleeping baby smugly, looks up, swishing her immaculate hair while staring at this spectacle. Just when I am about to burst into tears, I smell the unmistakable smell of baby poop.

Cursing my luck and wanting to take a parachute out of this plane, I struggle to get her diaper bag out of the overhead compartment, lug her to the bathroom, pull down her pants and . . . surprise, surprise . . . her diaper is clean as a whistle.

We come back to our seat and as the smell of

fetid broccoli gets worse, I again pull her pants agape and peer inside. Nope, not a thing. And then it hits me: It's the other baby next to us. Can the mother not smell it? It's the grossest, most familiar scent to all us poor women who go through raising little monsters into semi-decent adults.

I keep staring at the other mom hoping she gets on with it, but to no avail. I try to chew mint in the hope that it will get the smell out of my nose. Nope, that doesn't work either. Finally, just when I am about to give up, the woman starts sniffing around and, after peering at me—in what could be the longest 'your baby vs mine' stand-

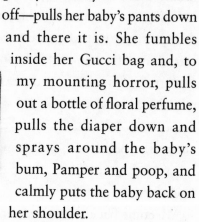

off—pulls her baby's pants down and there it is. She fumbles inside her Gucci bag and, to my mounting horror, pulls out a bottle of floral perfume, pulls the diaper down and sprays around the baby's bum, Pamper and poop, and calmly puts the baby back on her shoulder.

All right, so now I am sitting in an aromatic cloud of shit and Chanel No 5.

Whoever said 'Life is about the journey, not the destination' needs to sit like me—covering my head with the in-flight vomit bag for the rest of the journey, while desperately awaiting my destination—before they spout some more philosophy. Au revoir!

HOW DO YOU GET BACK INTO YOUR JEANS POST THE BABY?

Diligently try them on every month. At first, they will go just up your knee; then a month later, a bit higher and with each month that passes, they will go higher and higher, till they reach the ideal fit, whereby you lie down on your bed and pull the zip up.

Don't fret about it. After all, the best things in life are often done while lying flat on your back.

S: SO WHAT'S CHANGED, MOMMY?

MUSINGS OF A MIDDLE-AGED, NEW MOM

1. My bedtime: 8 p.m. was the time I would be relaxing with a glass of wine and planning what I am going to wear to tonight's event. Now, this is the time I am fast asleep in my bed, drooling in an exhaustion-induced coma.

2. My various body parts: Sometimes I think the only thing keeping them in place is delusion.

3. My clothes: Will I ever wear my J Brand size 26 again? And more importantly, do I have any clothes free of baby vomit to wear today?

4. My man: From gazing at me worshipfully and declaring how beautiful I am, he now has one term to compliment me no matter what I wear: Cute! What the hell is cute? Am I a bloody teddy bear?

5. My brains: With an enviable tested IQ of 145, now there are days when I can barely remember what rhymes with twinkle. Sparkle? Spangle?

6. My peer group: I have always had savvy thirty-something-year-old friends, but now I find myself conversing with twenty-four-year-old other new moms, only to wonder if I was as dumb at that age.

7. My home: I have always had an immaculate, elegant home, but gone are the days when my

living room could be featured in *Architectural Digest*; now it's difficult to even find my sofa under mounds of diapers, swaddle cloths, burp cloths and bibs.

8. My food: My regular diet of dainty salads and grilled chicken is banned from my meal plans, as my mother-in-law is now force-feeding me ladoos, dry fruits and ghee-infused bajra rotis to increase my fluid output. I am secretly starting to think that this fluid output nonsense is just an excuse she has made up to make sure I never lose any weight.

9. My status: The man of the house has very politely informed guests who have come to see the baby that I am unavailable, as I am 'milking', and thereby sealed my status from cool chick to mooing cow.

10. My outlook: My vanity has taken a hit and my brains have been sucker punched, but what has really changed is the way I look at this body—from groaning about each lump and bump, judging my body by my dress size, I now marvel at the strength of

this wonderful machine. It has produced two beautiful children, been terribly abused on occasion (apple martinis, anyone?), been neglected sometimes, but it has never let me down. Since it only responds to what I give it, with love, care, dedication and maybe a few starvation periods (let's not kid ourselves to the contrary), I will perhaps sashay in my old jeans once again, while simultaneously determining the exact square root of pi.

PEOPLE I WANT TO BOX ON THE HEAD

1. Box every woman I meet who talks about her bespoke handbags made in Paris and her monogrammed dustbins made in Milan—all in an accent that can only be made-in-Bombay, faked-in-Dubai and developed-in-Hong Kong.

2. Box people who undergo liposuction and then claim how they lost all their weight just by eating three healthy meals and two nutritious snacks every day.

3. Box watchmen, liftmen, postmen and other random men, who don't even say namaste the whole year round, but arrive early in the morning on Diwali, with a grin and a hand sticking out.

4. Box people who post minute-by-minute updates on Facebook depicting every detail of their December getaway. There are only so many 'Gee my life is wonderful' statuses that other people can bear.

T: TRAVEL AND TYRANNY

8 a.m.: I am in a little, relatively unknown town in Germany; it's an idyllic seaside small town where everyone knows everyone else and nothing seems to change. We come here almost every year or two to get the man of the house fit and ready to grapple with crocodiles and jump off skyscrapers.

10.30 a.m.: Waiting at the hospital for our turn in the physiotherapy department, I see a lot of people on crutches coming by as well. Each one limps in, calls out 'morgen' (morning in German) and everyone already sitting there answers back 'morgen'; by the forty-third 'morgen' that I have had to cheerfully force out of my mouth, I want to put one leg out and trip the next limping soldier that walks in.

I do notice something that is rather strange. In the waiting area, we are around fifty people, all (besides us) over sixty-five and not one person has anyone accompanying them to the hospital.

In India this never happens—there is always someone to take you to the hospital. Even if your children live far away, there will be cousins, buas, chachis, even neighbours; someone always steps in. Looking at these old people shuffling along by themselves, all I can say is: We may have potholed roads but at least we have many people willing to travel with us on them.

3 p.m.: We decide to go to the nearest city, which is Hamburg, and I cajole an extremely reluctant man of the house to take a bus tour with me. In the movie business, we travel the world, but all we really see are our mirrors, hotel rooms and

the shooting locations; so now that showbiz is far behind me, I am determined to see the world the way I should have all these years.

3.30 p.m.: We are sitting on the upper deck of the tour bus and our first destination is the red-light district of Hamburg. As the geriatric men in the bus are craning their necks, I make a few phone calls and get yelled at by my rotund, red-faced German tour guide, and am asked to go sit in the basement.

I start correcting him that a basement technically means a dwelling underneath ground level and even if I go below the bus and lie down between the tyres, I still won't be in the basement, but the man of the house pulls my arm and uses this as a great excuse to end our city tour.

7.30 p.m.: The man of the house is not feeling too well and I decide to go down to the hotel restaurant by myself. It is a nice day and the restaurant is partially outdoor, so I decide to sit in the fresh air and enjoy a steak. I look around and see that almost every table is filled with people, most of whom have brought their dogs along for dinner. I like dogs, I have two German shepherds at home (pun totally not intended), and I wonder at their culture which is so different from ours, of bringing their pets everywhere with them.

There is a cute dog at the next table, and the owner, an older German lady, smiles at me politely and nods when I ask her if I can give her dog a piece of my steak. I throw the piece down and the dog gratefully laps it up, and before I know it, the German lady is telling me that if I don't want to eat my steak, I should give the whole thing to her dog.

I am not that hungry, so I cut a few bites, but suddenly my neighbour is giving me brisk instructions, 'No, cut zee piece smaller, make tinier!' I do my best and then she says, 'My dog doezn't eat salt, so pleaze suck ze pieces of steak, zhen feed her.'

So here I am, cutting my steak into bits, following instructions to make it tinier, popping each piece into my mouth, sucking the salt and finally feeding it to a dog.

I come up to the room in a fury and declare that I want to ban everything made in Germany, especially all these bossy Germans. The man of the house looks up from his iPad, sighs deeply and says, 'Okay, darling, throw out our Siemens fridge, sell the Mercedes, tear up your Deutsche Bank chequebook, quit eating Black Forest cake, burn my Hugo Boss suit and toss away your Montblanc pen.'

I am staring at him in horror, awe and shock. He has never displayed his expertise in the area of general knowledge prior to this, and I stutter and ask, 'Er . . . How do you know all these uhh . . . things are German and all?'

He smirks and says, 'You are not the only one who can use Google, you know?'

Crap! Columbus has finally discovered America.

THREE THINGS YOU NEED TO KNOW ABOUT DOCTORS

1. Doctors are shorter in real life: When you meet your gynaecologist at a party, he will always look shorter, till you realize that you normally see him when you are flat on your back and he is looming over between your legs.

2. Doctors deliberately acquire bad handwriting: Can anyone really read a doc's prescription clearly? I think it's a well-thought-out scheme. Dear doc can prescribe Lamictal in his terrible handwriting and if you collapse with a seizure, he can claim he had actually written Lamisil, a mere antifungal.

3. Doctors have no sense of humour: The poker-faced doc walks in and declares that I have to take two injections, so I will have to bear a total of two pricks; when I crack up, saying that I have seen quite a few pricks and two more won't make a difference, he is still as poker-faced.

U: UNDRESSED UNDER DURESS

8 a.m.: I am walking on the beach with my sister-in-law when she tells me that she knows a good acupuncturist. The gentleman is my mother-in-law's old friend and since I have been moaning about a frozen shoulder that is not responding to physiotherapy and she has a knee problem that is also not getting any better, perhaps it's time to try some alternative therapy.

11 a.m.: We have made an appointment to see the doctor. Amidst my giggles on discovering his

name is Dr Luv, we confirm our presence at his clinic at 4 p.m.

3.45 p.m.: We are standing outside Dr Luv's clinic. It is a dingy little building in the far-flung suburbs and before I can ring the bell, the door flies open and it's the good doctor himself.

4 p.m.: The clinic is deserted, barring the doctor and a young oriental boy who is sluggishly dusting the reception table.

We start giving Dr Luv our medical history and soon enough he leads us to two tiny rooms and tells us to undress so that he can start our treatment. We try telling him that he can just jab the needles in the required spots, but he gives us a big lecture about how, in acupuncture, one needs to heal and treat the entire body and not just the symptoms.

We are ushered into dilapidated, musty rooms. Through the wall, I whisper to my sister-in-law, 'Why do we have to undress? What if there are cameras here to secretly film us? Let's just find some excuse and run away.'

We decide to tell Dr Luv that I am unable to breathe, as I am allergic to mould and we will do the treatment some other time.

To our horror, the doctor looks unperturbed, and says, 'I will come to your house and do the treatment.'

I stutter, 'But your other patients? How can you leave them?'

'Don't worry!' he says and calls out to the boy who is now dusting some shelves, 'Aye, Nepali, listen! Kukreja will come at 5 p.m. for his treatment, *usko bees pachees sui ghusa dena*' (shove twenty–twenty-five needles into him).

The Nepali boy looks shocked and terrified, but meekly nods.

4.45 p.m.: I am driving as fast as I can, but each time I look in the rear-view mirror, I see Dr Luv still following us in his dilapidated 1984 maroon Mercedes. I tell my sis-in-law, 'God knows if the needles are sterilized! If we are forced to undergo this, at least let's get some new acupuncture needles.'

My sister-in-law swiftly makes a few calls, and lo and behold, has organized new acupuncture needles to be delivered to the house shortly.

5.35 p.m.: Dr Luv has unfortunately not lost his way, and unable to stall him any more, I get ready for the treatment the same way a prisoner gets ready for the guillotine. Just in time, my sister-in-law rushes into the room with the fresh needles and a remarkable excuse, 'Dr Luv, why don't you use these needles? Someone gave it to me on Diwali last year and it's just been lying here uselessly.'

I am staring at her aghast. What a daft excuse! Who gives anyone acupuncture needles for Diwali! Even Dr Luv looks shocked, but she thrusts the needles and her chest towards him, and it's a done deal.

7 p.m.: The treatment is over and I now have the answer to two mystical questions that I wouldn't even have thought of in the first place. What will happen to a human being who manages to fall

in between two porcupines trying to mate? And why do they say that acupuncture is a treatment done by pricks? Hmm . . . A bad pun hurts, but Luv definitely hurts more.

The prodigal son complained that for the school's Republic Day function, he was assigned the traumatic task of singing and dancing to 'India Waale'; his protests that singing the national anthem would be more appropriate had gone unheeded. Hmm . . . If he enters the family business, he will have to learn to dance to all sorts of inappropriate songs, so he might as well start now . . .

V: VICTORY LIES IN CUTTING YOUR LOSSES AND NOT YOUR WRISTS

TUESDAY

6 a.m.: The prodigal son is leaving for a school trip and, as usual, the weary, bleary-eyed parents are called to school at 8 a.m. to get a final briefing before the much-awaited trip, and that is the sole reason that I am all ready in jeans, a comfortable kurta and my flip-flops.

6.15 a.m.: My son looks at me in alarm and says, 'No way, Mom, you always wear this same kurta, you can't come to school like this! Wear that nice dress you wore to that birthday party!'

My son, unfortunately, like all men, has a vision of the perfect woman and since I am the only woman in his life right now, this vision is periodically foisted on me.

Comments from the recent past:

1. Your hair doesn't look nice, do that thing with that roller thing you have.

2. Can you wear a belt with that dress, you look pregnant.

3. Open your ponytail and bring your hair in front (this while playing badminton).

4. Why have you put so much lipstick? Red doesn't suit you, Mom.

5. Fix that button, Mom! You can't go out like this.

Sighing deeply, I ignore his comments and focus on thrusting vegetable juice down his throat, and we get into the car.

8 a.m.: The fifty-odd people in this room (including me) look like we are trying out for a part in the next season of *The Walking Dead,* but thankfully before we all start snoring in our chairs, the presentation starts.

The first slide comes on and as I am peering over the top of some freakishly tall father's head, I notice that the first line on the slide states that we have to drop our kids off on the 12th of January and pick them up on the 14th of November. Can the school really be kind enough to take our children off our hands for over ten months? Another parent who cannot resist the temptation to throw egg on the teacher's face, puts his hands up and points out the obvious, 'Oh, Miss, see in the board, it says 14th November. You make mistake like this?'

The poor teacher doesn't point out the grammatical mistakes in his statement, but simply reassures us that they are, in fact, taking our children for only five days, and gives us a long list of items to be packed.

THURSDAY

4 p.m.
Me: 'Have you packed your Vicks thermometer?'
Him: 'Mom, leave me alone, why are you obsessed with that thing!'

6 p.m.
Him: 'Mom, can I pack my pepper spray?'
Me: 'I don't think you will need it, the teachers are around you 24/7!'
Him: 'That's why I need it!'

8 p.m.
Him: 'Mom, I have packed my Swiss Army knife.'
Me: 'Why? Are you going on a school trip or trying to attack Afghanistan?'
Him: 'Mom, your jokes suck.'

SUNDAY

6.45 a.m.: We are driving to his football match. I start giving him tips on safety during the trip.

Everything from 'If you fall off the canoe and see a shark, don't panic' to 'Shake your shoes and clothes before wearing them in case an insect has crawled inside.'

Perhaps it's the morning air or the fact that we are driving alone on deserted roads, but the conversation takes its own route and I start telling him that when we were growing up, all we were told was, 'Try and try harder till you die' and today life is different, there is bravery in quitting, in not staying in one place for the sake of it. I ask him, 'What will you do if something doesn't work out?' He says, 'I will keep trying and never give up!' and I tell him, 'No, remember, the only person you can ever change is yourself; after you have done that and you are the best you that you can be, let go. There is always another job, another woman, another best friend. Each day that you persist in a situation where you are miserable is a day wasted on the path that would lead you to happiness.'

He looks at me and says, 'So you are saying I should take the easy way out?'

And I say, 'No, I want you to know the difference between trying and holding on.'

MONDAY

4.20 a.m.: The man of the house and I put his things in the car and we drive to the airport.

4.45 a.m.: The prodigal son sees his friends standing outside the airport, grabs his things and runs in excitement to his group. They start going inside and just before he goes in, he turns around and gives me a quick wave.

One day he will be in my place and what he will learn then is that trying and holding on are complicated and challenging things, but the most difficult thing in life is to love fiercely and then let go.

I muster a smile and blow him a kiss.

Godspeed.

SEVEN EMAILS IN MY INBOX THIS MORNING

No. 1: Kindly giving me a discount on Vacuum Penile Pumps.

No. 2: Informing me that I have won 3.2 million dollars in a lucky draw.

No. 3: Stating that I have been invited to judge a beauty contest at Friendship Club, in Patna.

No. 4: Saying 'Hi, Beta!' and has attachments of ugly pictures of me as a teenager. From mother . . .

No. 5: Forward requesting free poker chips. From mother . . .

No. 6: Pictures of a hideous cabinet. From mother . . .

No. 7: A link to a website where I can buy a card and get a 5 per cent discount at Kala Saris and Dress Materials. From mother . . .

W: WHERE ARE THE HOMING PIGEONS WHEN YOU NEED THEM?

7 a.m.: My phone makes a strangled sound and I stumble out of bed, groaning and holding my head. Last night, I had to brave the most fearsome animal of all: the quintessential Bollywood party, and in order to stand still in the eye of this hurricane, I took a two-pronged approach to retain my sanity.

1. A five-minute yoga session before leaving for the party to align my body, soul and mind.

2. Five drinks down my throat after reaching the party to delude myself into thinking that I am funnier and smarter than I truly am.

7.05 a.m.: My phone pings again and I see eight WhatsApp forwards about love and kindness. I wonder if on a Sunday morning all these enthusiastic do-gooders could send out truly helpful things like '11 cures for a hangover' or 'How to clean puke stains from your dress'. I have no such luck; all I get are strange messages like 'Little memories can last for years'. Very useful when you are trying hard to forget all the embarrassing things you did the night before.

Do I really need messages saying, 'A little hug can wipe out a big tear' or 'Friendship is a rainbow'?

There is also a message saying, 'God blues you', which I am trying to guess could mean that either God wants to bless me, rule me or make a blue movie with me.

Has it ever happened that a murderer just before committing

his crime gets a message stating, 'Life is about loving', and stops in his tracks, or a banker reads 'No greater sin than cheating', and quits his job?

So, what do these messages really do? I think they allow lazy people to think that they are doing a good deed in the easiest possible manner by sending these daft bits of information out into the universe.

Go out there! Sweep a pavement, plant a tree, feed a stray dog. Do something, anything; rather than just using your fingers to tap three keys and destroy 600 people's brain cells in one shot.

11 a.m.: This is turning out to be a hectic day. The work that I have to accomplish seems to range from begging the dentist to see our son who has managed to break part of his braces on a Sunday morning (why can't these children choose a Tuesday or Thursday to mangle themselves is beyond me) to getting the baby ready for her friend's birthday party.

I spend half an hour wrapping the present artistically with contrasting bows, because I am obsessed with silly things like gift wrapping rather than serious matters like 'Did Kiran Bedi really tow the PM's car?'

1 p.m.: I am peering at grocery bills written half in Hindi, with a few gibberish English words, and the rest in what could be Swahili, when I start seeing messages on my iPhone like, 'Oh, t she is so cute, I just saw on Facebook.' Wondering if my friend has seen the picture I posted of a French coffee cup and has decided to forgo the rules of grammar, I ignore it and go back to my bills.

Ping! Another message, 'She looks just like you ringlets and all.'

Time to investigate . . .

I go to my Facebook page and in sheer horror discover that there is a video of the baby and me posted on my page.

FLASHBACK: 9 a.m.: The baby is running around in her grandmother's house, she is snatching my lime juice, she is throwing peanuts at my mother-in-law, she is rattling the TV remote, she is climbing on our dog—in other words, she is driving me crazy, and in order to calm her down I give her my phone.

END RESULT: She has randomly jabbed a few buttons, managed to hit bull's eye and posted this video on Facebook where I am in my eleven-year-old nightgown with toothpaste in my hair, holding the saintly looking (Dr Jekyll and Mr Hyde) baby, pointing at the camera, and saying, 'Show me your belly button . . . Show me your belly button' again and again.

If the man of the house ever wants sole custody of the children, he can produce this video in court to prove that I am unstable, on drugs, and undisputedly deranged.

I quickly delete the video, but not before 720 people have seen it on my (so far only work related) 'The White Window' page.

4 p.m.: I am driving by Juhu and I see a beautiful peacock perching on a rusty building gate. I frantically point him out to the baby, bring my car to a screeching halt and whip out my phone to take a sublime photo of this extremely unusual

moment, only to find that my memory is full as I have just received twenty-eight WhatsApp images from my cousin Kamalnath (Sweetie) Khanna.

5 p.m.: I have now formulated my own WhatsApp forward message which I am going to send to my entire contact list, and it goes like this: 'Dear Sir/Madam, I have recently been diagnosed with Systematic Psychotic Urge Disorder (SPUD), and random forwards seem to worsen my condition. Please help me save the planet one person at a time. God blues you.'

7 p.m.: I am in the gym frantically trying to undo last week's cupcake damage when I get an SMS from the man of the house, stating, 'I am on my way home.'

I quickly call him because he left for Nepal this morning and am pretty sure he was supposed to be there for a week. He answers the phone, snorts and says, 'I sent you that message yesterday!'

7.04 p.m.: I finish my phone call only to realize that while I was talking, my iPhone has managed to dial and redial Inspector Bapat at Juhu police station 44 times for no rhyme or reason, and before I get arrested for harassing the police, I quickly switch my phone off.

9 p.m.: After in-depth analysis I have come to the conclusion that God was right when he told Adam to leave the apple alone, and I, too, decide to give up apples, blackberries and any other new fruits of technology, and from now on communicate only through homing pigeons.

I pulled your little pigtail,
It was as curly as my dog's tail,
I had to leave mom's shirt tail,
It's a vagary I cannot curtail.

X: XEROX COPY OF MOM REQUIRED

A few years ago, at the ripe old age of seven, the prodigal son brought home a girl. She was a bit plump, a bit bossy and a bit aggressive, and reminded me of someone, though I couldn't quite put my finger on it.

She would drop by for play dates twice a week, and things were going along splendidly till one fine day, while I was washing the prodigal son's hair, with soap suds all over his eyes, he decided to enlighten me with the fact that he is in love.

A few seconds later, I was flat on my back on the bathroom floor. Since this is not a black-and-white Hindi movie, I had not, in fact, suffered a heart attack, but had merely slipped on the bar of soap which had fallen out of my hand in shock at this pronouncement.

Meanwhile, he continued chattering away. 'She is very nice, Mom, and she is just like you. She also talks to me the way you talk to dad—"Come here right now! Do this just now!"'

I feebly muttered, 'I don't really talk like this and uh . . . I do yoga and stuff, so . . . I am not bossy any more.'

Visions of having a mini-me daughter-in-law started swimming in my brain, and I hurriedly continued, 'I think you should find girls like granny; she is so kind and nice, no?'

He paused for a moment, gave me a fierce glare and continued, 'I don't like girls like granny, and I like Mina because she is just like you.'

A few days passed and just like any grown-up relationship, a few problems started creeping up between them as well.

Like . . .

1. She doesn't like his cousin and has told him not to bring her to any of the birthday parties that they attend.

2. She doesn't like the fact that when they were playing together, his grandmother came to visit and he jumped up, hugged his granny and said how happy he was to see her.

3. She doesn't like his mother and has questioned him as to why he was sitting next to his mother and sucking on a lollipop when he should have been on the swing with her.

4. She doesn't like him playing with his camera and has nagged him so much about it that he promptly took his camera and locked himself in the bathroom and refused to come out till she left.

Though this would have been enough to push married people to seek divorce courts, in their world of bubble gum and candyfloss, these were just minor hiccups.

Their love story came to an abrupt end when my pudgy seven-year-old nemesis had to leave Mumbai with her family for greener pastures.

As she packed her bags and he made her a goodbye card, I opened a bottle of champagne and heaved a sigh of relief.

So, if you find your son in love with a little Hitler in pigtails, there is not much you can do except step out of the way, go to holy places, fast on alternate Fridays and desperately pray that by some cosmic force, her father is immediately transferred to a destination so remote that even Google Maps is bewildered as to its whereabouts.

FOUR PEOPLE YOU BUMP INTO AT INDIAN FUNERALS

1. **The deceased's cousin's daughter's niece's cousin:** This is the individual who will wail the loudest, have intermittent fainting spells and will despondently narrate two sentimental incidents about the expired relative who incidentally she had met just once.

2. **The kleptomaniac:** She comes to the prayer meeting in her Bata slippers, and leaves wearing someone else's Gucci sandals.

3. **The daughter-in-law:** This is the poor soul who does all the running around and sees to it that all's in place, while answering umpteen questions as to when she will produce a bonny boy.

4. **Old aunties:** They have lived so long that now they have a wardrobe that consists only of funeral wear, as everyone they know seems to die weekly. They will watch the proceedings stoically, and will discreetly look at each other, wondering whose turn it is next.

Y: YOUNG UNDERDOGS

At the start of 1989, we lived in a bursting-at-the-seams joint-family-style house with eleven loosely related members of the family and one big dog. This tribe was lorded over by my formidable grandmother. She threw dollops of love and food our way and kept trying to drive the dog, Caesar, away.

She disliked the dog severely because he never got toilet trained and walked around our house as if it were one giant commode. Monthly arguments between my sister—a true lover of all sorts of hairy creatures—and granny—a probable hater of all sorts of hairy creatures—ensued about the fate of the dog, which only led to her hating the dog even more and being unable to do anything about it.

A year later, my aunt separated from her Sardar husband and came back to live with us. She did not come back alone and thus Jimmy was introduced into our lives.

Jimmy's parents were related to my aunt's ex-husband and though they lived in Jalandhar, they felt that little Jimmy would have a better life in Mumbai with his distant relatives. My aunt developed a great fondness for him and soon he became part of her household, and when she left her marital home, in a bizarre chain of events, Jimmy was the only alimony she brought along.

He was a spritely six-year-old turbaned wonder and just another odd creature added to our strange cauldron, and because I was in junior college (which is the time of one's life when one does absolutely nothing), certain responsibilities were foisted on me. Namely, looking after Jimmy's homework and taking him swimming twice a week to the local club.

He taught me Punjabi, I taught him some English, and life went on. I vaguely remember making him and my sister coat our neighbour's car with such a thick layer of wet mud that not a speck of its original gleaming metal was visible.

And then there were our swimming sessions— getting him lessons at the club and then forcing him to do laps, finally chasing him out of the pool, a quick shower and a rickshaw ride back home.

One fine afternoon, we were both in the ladies shower room, bathing with our swimsuits on, as part of our daily routine. I scrubbed his Rapunzel-like hair in the shower cubicle and, as he was rinsing off, I started shampooing my own. In less than a minute, I heard two piercing shrieks. I opened my eyes and looked around frantically, only to realize that Jimmy had slid in the gaps between cubicles and had emerged three cubicles to the left, where a Parsi lady was showering in the buff. A wizened-looking boy with waist-length hair semi-plastered on his face, popping up suddenly while you are scrubbing your armpits would scare even the bravest of us.

An angry complaint was duly filed against Jimmy and his neglectful guardian, and we were both barred from the club for a month.

All was well except my granny had a slight aversion to this hairy creature as well. She was fed up of cleaning his sandwich crumbs from  her bedside table, of weekly combing through his long, stringy hair looking for lice and of making sure he was suitably fed during the hours my aunt was working.

She never voiced her disapproval, but all the muttering under her breath made her feelings about the Jimmy situation loud and clear. As was inevitable, the two underdogs in the family, one of the canine variety and the other of the Sardar variety, trudged a remarkable alliance and my sister was part of this strange group as well.

Time went by. Jimmy lost a few milk teeth and grew a few others back.

He would sit on the porch on weekends and take out Caesar's ticks and my granny would be reluctantly combing through his hair, looking for blood suckers of another variety. Not much would have changed this equation, till her beloved niece Masooma, all the way from Texas, came to attend a funeral, but ended up staying with us for a fortnight.

Masooma would grab her Cadbury, a Mills & Boon and a pillow, and head straight to the hammock tied between two trees in our garden, every evening at 4, and tumble out of her reading nook only two hours later.

One day as she was lying in the hammock on a rather windy day, Caesar went up to her and started barking, and would not stop. Hearing the din, Jimmy and my sister came out to the garden. I scrambled out of my room as well to join my granny who was standing on the porch; she was livid at what she perceived as yet another annoyance caused by this motley crew that were now disturbing her precious NRI relative.

Caesar leaped towards the hammock, and Jimmy, thinking that he was about to attack Masooma, yanked her arm so hard that all three of them tumbled four feet away from the hammock into the grass.

My granny screamed in fury, and just as she took two steps, the monsoon wind, in a furious gust, managed to break a massive tree branch, which landed exactly on the hammock.

Everyone was in shock. Visions of Masooma getting crushed by the branch were running through our minds. My granny gave Jimmy the tightest hug ever. Caesar was declared a visionary dog that could foretell that Masooma was in grave danger and had thus barked his lungs out to save her. Of course, he was bequeathed the status of a hero.

Just like a blockbuster movie, the underdogs had triumphed, an evil cosmic force had been vanquished and a maiden had been rescued.

I wish I could say that they lived happily ever after, but two months after Masooma went back to Texas, things went back to normal. The invisible bravery medals bestowed on Caesar and

Jimmy were taken away as Caesar decided to bite the dhobi, and Jimmy threw up on my granny's brother. Thus, both of them were soon relegated to their previous positions.

MORAL OF THE STORY: Your greatest moment in life soon joins a series of other moments and is often forgotten. As you rise, so shall you eventually fall.

A MOM IS A WEIRD CREATURE

Me: 'Listen, everyone is tired and it's really hot, let's go back home.'

Son: 'You never do anything for me, you only love the baby. I just want to stay in the pool for one hour more.'

Me: 'Little monster, don't pull this sympathy card on me. Your dad may get fooled, but I know you.'

Son: 'Stop! Ok! Let's go back, just don't give me your usual, "I know you, I gave birth to you. You are flesh of my flesh, blood of my blood." Who even talks like that? You are so weird, Mom!'

Z: ZIP YOUR MOUTH FOR GOD'S SAKE

8 a.m.: Today is Raksha Bandhan, an ancient festival where a sister ties a rakhi (sacred thread) on her brother's wrist. This symbolizes the bond between them. The sister prays for her brother's well-being and the brother promises to protect her from all harm.

One of the legendary stories about rakhi involves Rani Karnavati, the widow of the king of Chittor, who sent a rakhi to emperor Humayun so that he would refrain from invading her kingdom.

No, I didn't know all of this, but have looked it up just to answer the million questions that my children are bound to ask me. There are times when they ask me things that I don't have an answer to, like 'But what is blue?', or 'If God is everywhere, so when I do potty, am I doing potty on Him?' However, for the queries that do have some sort of an answer, I like to be thoroughly prepared.

10 a.m.: The baby is struggling to tie a rakhi onto her brother's wrist; the brother keeps muttering that having a shiny orange thread with a picture of a bare-chested Salman Khan wrapped around his wrist is just not cool.

This is apparently my fault because I called Vinod Book Store (a shop that can supply seasonal decorations, pens, wrapping paper; anything besides the books that it claims to sell on its billboard) and requested them to send one of their bestselling rakhis, and I got this in return. Well, it seems Salman really is everyone's favourite bhai.

10.30 a.m.: My phone rings and it's mummyji who informs me that six of her real brothers, two not-real brothers (are they imaginary?) and hordes of cousins are coming over this evening. I am then enlightened with the fact that I must have some snacks ready for them and that I should wear that pretty orange salwar kameez that she gave me as a surprise gift last week.

11 a.m.: The man of the house, who also has a real sister and thirteen cousins, has asked me to have gifts ready for the entire brigade. He sees the saris I have picked out for them and says that I am being miserly and stingy, and that I should get them all jewellery instead.

Oh great karmic force, if I miraculously get reincarnated as a woman again instead of a spider or a dog flea, then let me be born as one of the man of the house's sisters. They float in and out of the house as they please; my mother-in-law showers love and money on each of them and they get precious gems for rakhi; whereas all I get is the wonderful title of being an all-round dogsbody.

1.30 p.m.: Mommy dearest sent an antique door to my house yesterday despite me protesting that I already have enough doors to enter all the rooms in my house.

I am now looking at this monstrosity which my desi Jeeves has propped in front of my cupboard and wondering how I am supposed to get dressed at all.

1.50 p.m.: The antique door has been pushed out of the way and my wardrobe is once again at my disposal. I pull out the orange salwar kameez and it does not fit.

Either I have lost tons of weight, or more likely, this was given as a gift to my mother-in-law, and not being worthy of adorning her fine form, she simply passed it on to me. Well, to give her the benefit of the doubt, at least it's my favourite colour and I can always get it altered by 156 inches all over.

6 p.m.: I can't cook but since my philosophy in life is based on never revealing my weaknesses to my in-laws, I have called Nature's Basket and asked them to deliver seekh kebabs and samosas that need to be put in boiling oil for three minutes and are then ready to serve. A minute saved is a minute that can be used for useful things, like weighing myself for the fourteenth time that week.

6.30 p.m.: The prodigal son has decided that we must at least fry these snacks ourselves and has banished our cook from his domain. He has a lot of training from his father and, unlike me, is quite handy in the kitchen. Often on a Saturday morning, he makes French toast with sprinkled cinnamon, and I am rather proud of his culinary skills.

The oil is boiling in the pan and the kitchen is stuffy. Getting rather irritated with the heat, I start grumbling about how we Indians always have to make enough food to feed an army and how Indians have so many festivals that are always about food; the prodigal son interrupts me and asks, 'But, Mom, what does it really mean to be Indian?'

I don't even pause for a beat and start reciting, 'We are an ancient race of optimists, who hold our past firmly while we walk into the future. We have nuclear power reactors, but still believe in the power of black threads encircling our wrists. We have such strong family bonds that even if someone is just going to the train station, there will be eleven people, all loaded up in a tempo to accompany him and we . . .'

But he looks up at me and says, 'No, Mom, tell me what you really think. I know the way you speak, this weird zombie tone is the same one you use to answer people when they ask you which is your favourite temple or what you love cooking! Tell me the truth.'

'All right,' I say, 'if you want an honest answer, then Made in India is just a label coded in your genes. It is random chance that one is born within certain man-made boundaries, or is of a certain race, or of a certain religion, nothing more. So how does being born this side of a border or the other make any group of people better than another group? If God exists, then I doubt if He prefers people on the basis of their knowing Sanskrit or Urdu or English or Ger . . .'

The prodigal son gets all bug-eyed and screeches, 'What?' he splutters. 'What do you mean if God exists? God is not real? You have never said this before, Mom!'

Holy cow! My brain has been spinning with so many thoughts that I absolutely forgot to evaluate my words before throwing them all out in the air.

All these years I haven't voiced my opinions (well, a few sarcastic remarks may have slipped through) out of respect for his father's beliefs, and my respect for the prodigal son himself that he should grow up and form his own convictions rather than have mine foisted on him. Now here I am, in this hot, sticky kitchen, waving away flies from the samosas and having to finally confess that it's not just the rituals that I don't see sense in, but also the main guy Himself.

I take a deep breath and finally all I say is this, 'I just think that people rely too much on God; instead of asking to be in God's favour, I would rather stack the odds in my favour. At the very least, I am certain that I exist. But ask your dad all these questions, you know I am not the religious type.'

He looks up at me with his big blue eyes (his and her recessive genes in perfect alignment) and says, 'Mom, you know what? You should write a book about what all you think, all this cool stuff about borders and all.'

I swing my mosquito racquet like I am playing in the Grand Slam finals, demolish a fly about to sit on my samosas, and say, 'Perhaps someday I will.'

8 p.m.: Everyone has gathered at my mother-in-law's home. There are old Hindi songs playing and everywhere you look people are munching on jalebis and tikkas, and chatting away. A large group in the corner is busy playing housie. The man of the house is in charge of the proceedings and each number is announced in a whimsical manner, 'Eight and eight, two uncles on a date!'

I am introduced to my sister-in-law's new rakhi brother which in today's day and age probably means: I like you a little and also find you a bit creepy, thus have no intention of fornicating with you, but I need another relative, as my twenty-eight relatives are not enough to celebrate our 168 festivals.

9.30 p.m.: The prodigal son is gently holding his baby sister's hand as he navigates between cousins and friends. Sometimes when I look at them from a distance, I try and squint my eyes and clear my mind. I peer at them the way a stranger would—without any emotions, just observations. In this large fortress I had created around my heart, the one that let me enter situations easily and leave even more easily, how did they find a cat flap that allowed them to crawl into my soul?

As is inevitable, while I am doing my squinting business, a bulky aunty has managed to trip over another relative who is known only as Chota Vijay. Yes, he is short and no, he doesn't feel terrible about his nickname. Auntyji has not only tripped over him, but has splattered her kesar lassi on me.

A perfect end to my perfect day and this is just the excuse I need to make a hasty exit.

Just as I am about to leave, I spot my mother-

231

in-law munching on my samosas with her six real and two not-imaginary brothers. She is playing cards on a little table with them and I can hear them chattering in Punjabi and cackling away.

Her ways are different from mine; she treats me like her daughter on most days and like her daughter-in-law on a few others, but she has the ability to pull the whole family together and create gatherings like this effortlessly and sometimes I envy that.

I linger near the door. I have to pack for an early morning flight tomorrow to yet another trade fair and the sour smell of lassi is wafting through my hair, but I still linger.

I watch them like I have from the beginning, an oddball in this world of traditions and rituals. And as I continue dilly-dallying, the man of the house calls out, 'Oye, where you going? Stay for a while and dance with us, na.'

Do I want to go back to my factual, functional world or linger on in their saffron-coloured, cardamom-scented cosmos that resounds with bhangra and dholak?

I am a misfit here, like most women that enter

families which are so different from theirs. But I keep these thoughts to myself and stay. And for the next few hours, matching all the cousins, step for step, I make my own little place.

Will I inhabit this spot in perpetuum? I am not sure, but right now, with a string of borrowed jasmine flowers wrapped around my bun to mask the smell of yogurt, and my dupatta fluttering in the draught from the creaky air conditioner, I dance to the drumbeats and the night slips away.

ACKNOWLEDGEMENTS

I would like to thank my dear husband for reading every word that I have ever written. You are the diesel in my Innova, the helium in my balloon, and the ice cube in my apple martini.

A big hug to my sister for trying to make everything I write politically correct and for suffering through my 'Just read and tell me what you think?' moments time and again.

Thank you, mommy, for being so uniquely magnificent, everything I am is because of you.

My mother-in-law and sister-in-law, thank you for being wonderful women, and for always being there for me.

A big hug to Aarav and Nitara, my heart bursts with joy just by being around you two.

Sarita Tanwar, by persuading me to write that

first column, you opened up the barn door and all the chickens ran out into the meadow, so thank you, my friend.

Thank you, Pritish Nandy, for some solid advice and for lending me your ear and your shoulder as well. This was your idea.

A shout-out to my *Sunday Times* editor, Neelam Raaj, for all her support.

A big thank you to Gaurav Shrinagesh and the great team at Penguin Random House. Milee Ashwarya for making it all happen, Aparajita Ninan, Shanuj V.C., Aman Arora and Caroline Newbury, thank you for making all of this real.

And finally, I am eternally grateful to my editor, Chiki Sarkar, for her kind, but ruthless advice. I would not have written this book if it weren't for you.